THE ECONOMICS OF THE
SINGLE EUROPEAN ACT

SOUTHAMPTON SERIES IN INTERNATIONAL ECONOMICS

General Editor: George McKenzie, Director, Centre for International Economics, University of Southampton, England

The Centre for International Economics at the University of Southampton was established in 1987 with a view to achieving two objectives: firstly, to undertake research into economic issues of contemporary significance for Britain and its wider role in the European and world economy; secondly, to communicate the results of this research in a manner that is accessible to the educated layman whether involved in the business, financial or government sectors. The series is one of the means which the Centre will utilise to communicate the results of its investigations.

Published titles

Sven Arndt and George McKenzie (editors)
THE COMPETITIVENESS OF THE UK ECONOMY

George McKenzie and Stephen Thomas
FINANCIAL INSTABILITY AND THE INTERNATIONAL DEBT PROBLEM

George McKenzie and Anthony J. Venables (*editors*)
THE ECONOMICS OF THE SINGLE EUROPEAN ACT

The Economics of the Single European Act

Edited by
George McKenzie

Director
Centre for International Economics,
University of Southampton

and

Anthony J. Venables

Eric Roll Professor of Economic Policy
University of Southampton

Foreword by
Alexis Jacqemin

M IN ASSOCIATION WITH THE
CENTRE FOR INTERNATIONAL ECONOMICS
UNIVERSITY OF SOUTHAMPTON

First published 1991

Published by
MACMILLAN ACADEMIC AND PROFESSIONAL LTD
Houndmills, Basingstoke, Hampshire RG21 2XS
and London
Companies and representatives
throughout the world

Printed in Great Britain by Billing & Sons Ltd, Worcester

British Library Cataloguing in Publication Data
The Economics of the Single European Act.
1. European Community countries. Economic integration
I. McKenzie, George   II. Venables, Anthony J.   III.
University of Southampton, *Centre for International
Economics*
337.142
ISBN 0–333–54685–7

Contents

List of Tables

List of Figures

List of Abbreviations

BIS	Bank for International Settlements
CEN	Comité Européen des Normes
DIN	Deutsche Industrie-Norm
EC	European Community/Commission
ECU	European Currency Unit
EFTA	European Free Trade Association
EMCF	European Monetary Co-operation Fund
EMS	European Monetary System
ERM	Exchange Rate Mechanism
FT	*The Financial Times*
GATT	General Agreement on Tariffs and Trade
GDP	Gross Domestic Product
GNP	Gross National Product
ISO	International Standards Organisation
MTFS	Medium Term Financial Strategy
NIC	Newly industrialised country
NTB	Non-tariff barrier
OJEC	*Official Journal of the European Community*
SEA	Single European Act
VAT	Value added tax
VER	Voluntary export restraint
VSTF	Very short-term financing

Foreword

Alexis Jacqemin

'The economics of the Single European Act' is a complex matter, not easily understood through traditional approaches to economics and political science.

First the emerging large internal market will not even approximate traditional textbook models. After the promised liberalisation in Europe, intra-EC trade will still be affected by extensive product differentiation, complex production technologies, incomplete information and various forms of collusive or non-collusive oligopolistic behaviour. The source of these imperfections lies in the exogenous characteristics of the demand and cost functions, as well as in the strategies adopted by private and public agents. And in fact the major part of the potential gains from completing the internal market relies on the very existence of such features.

Second, the related institutional, regulatory and public policy framework will not correspond to a clear-cut system with well-identified historical counterparts, but looks more like a (fragile) prototype. Progress towards deregulation in 1992 is an essential key to the large internal market and the directives that form the heart of the project must be incorporated as soon as possible into national laws and put into practice. But since the ratification of the Single European Act, the EC members are committed to much more than completing the common market. The progressive realisation of an economic and monetary union, the development of the social dimension of the Community and the implementation of a European foreign policy imply a far greater surrender of national sovereignty than what is implicit in a single market and will lead to some form of organisation closer to a political union.

Given such a complex design, it is necessary to employ a multiplicity of economic and socio-political analyses in order to bring to light the crucial issues at stake and the risks entailed in this structural reform. Preliminary reflections can illustrate some of these issues.

Concerning the potential gains, several sources have been identified besides direct cost-saving through lower real trade costs: greater production efficiency achieved thanks to the enlargement of the market, reduction in monopoly power in national markets leading to reallocation of resources from highly to less competitive industries, and, generally, but not always, an enlargement of the range and diversity of available products and services. The point to note here is that these gains from trade liberalisation rely on the existence of imperfect competition and are additional to those expected in competitive markets, so that the classical arguments for free trade are strengthened.

Predictions must be given about the evaluation of these effects. First, the gains from scale economies are viewed as not negligible, especially in some sectors such as railway equipment or telecommunications and computing equipment, in some stages of the value-added chain such as in the production of standard components and sub-assemblies, and in some countries, especially the newer member states. However, the European Commission does not give great weight to the general argument in favour of larger size and mergers and has indeed expressed strong scepticism about the existence of scale economies in many industries, including services.

Second, a more homogenous European product market is not expected; on the contrary, a broader range of products will be encouraged by extended geographic coverage. In fact a broader market, as well as more flexible production methods, could allow better exploitation of scale economies while preserving or increasing diversity in final goods.

Third, several potential gains of the completion of the internal market have not been quantified because of a lack of reliable information. One crucial aspect is the long-term growth effects of 1992. According to traditional growth theory, long-term per capita growth is determined entirely by exogenous technological change. But new theories suggest that competition, market size and trade policy can affect growth rates. To the extent that the marginal product of capital depends on the total amount of factors employed, the long-term growth effect of 1992 might be significant.

Whatever the plausibility of these speculations, we observe today some signals suggesting that the 1992 programme has successfully raised business expectations. Over the period 1987–8, there has been:

(a) a private investment boom in the EC, with a 7 per cent increase in gross private capital formation, mainly creating new capacity;

(b) an 85 per cent rate of capacity utilisation in industry, a high point not reached since 1975;
(c) a net creation of more than 2 millions jobs;
(d) a sharp increase in the intensity of intra-EC trade;
(e) a GNP growth rate of more than 3 per cent.

Furthermore, various indicators show a process of strategic integration of European business operations. Restructuring leads to less product diversification and broader geographical coverage facilitated by more flexible and less costly transportation and distribution within the EC. Companies such as Kodak, Unilever, Petrofina and Ferrero are replacing multiple national and regional locations by Euro-centralised production, stocking and marketing networks. The present wave of mergers, takeovers and divestiture reflects a rapid implementation of these strategies, and intra-European transactions of this type are increasingly frequent. Similar moves are observed in the financial services sector where national markets have hitherto been heavily protected and regulated. Non-EC multinational firms are also multiplying their direct investments within the EC, probably stimulated by the growth of EC markets and the expected competitive advantages of such a location compared to pure national strategies, exports or direct investment in other third countries.

Such developments, however, leave open several major questions. To what extent is this process of expansion sustainable? How is it possible to sustain sufficient credibility for the 1992 programme so that firms may place reasonable reliance on their future business environment evolving in the expected way? What is the role of accompanying policies intended to regulate the competitive process and avoid various perverse effects? Finally to what extent will political commitments be maintained and/or strengthened?

No simple answers can be given to these questions, mainly because the 1992 programme is not just a venture in deregulation. Most of the 300 directives listed in the EC's 1985 'White Paper' are intended to create an economic space in which goods, services, people and capital can move without barriers. And indeed deregulation is on its way in many domains, such as telecommunications, transport, product standards and financial services. But a strengthening of the EC capacity for coordination and policy management is also crucial given the existing high level of interdependence and the corresponding substantial amount of transnational externalities that can be internalised, in fields such as environment and consumer protection, competition and macroeconomic policy. Completing the internal market will accentuate these factors, at least for certain types of activity. Furthermore, the challenge of 1992 is not just economic, it is also political and social. Accepting the corresponding social and political costs implies a greater solidarity among the member states.

There is considerable uncertainy about the right balance between overall deregulation and regulation, and this uncertainty reflects the absence of an explicit consensus among the EC members, not only about the means to sustain the process of integration, but also about what the precise institutional destination should be in the construction of Europe.

This is especially evident from the debate stimulated by the 'Delors Committee report' outlining steps towards economic and monetary union and according to which in stage 3 the Federal European Monetary Institution would determine and execute monetary policy for the Community, in almost the same way as a federally organised central bank would at the national level.

The set of essays that George McKenzie and Tony Venables have selected for this volume provide stimulating illustrations of these issues and avoid simplistic choices between a naïve *laissez-faire* philosophy and a bureaucratic system of supranational regulations. They suggest, on the contrary, that a dialectic approach is necessary, striving to create 'diversity with safety', 'competition with cooperation', 'efficiency with equity and solidarity'.

The combination of completing the internal market and linked systemic developments in domains such as regional, technological, fiscal and monetary policy demands a gradual restructuring of the institutional framework within which policies are set and corporate strategies are elaborated. Such is the case of EC competition policy. If the positive effects of the completion of the internal market are to materialise, the competitive process must be maintained, in order to control the dangers of increased concentration in private and public operations and to prevent an intensification of direct and indirect government interventions to safeguard a policy of national champions. This is especially so when domestic market power is largely exercised at the expense of foreign consumers and to the benefit of national producers. That is why the European authorities have decided that, simultaneously with the liberalisation of markets, there must be a reinforcement of the control of mergers and takeovers and stricter control of public subsidies paid to companies.

Another crucial concern is the complex link between the allocative and the distributive effects of increased integration. Although the probability of substantial allocative gains is high, numerous equity problems exist: freedom of movement of labour, confirmed in 1988 by an agreement on a comprehensive formula subjecting all professions to the principle of mutual recognition, might increase the incentives for coordinated regional policies aimed at improving the skill composition of labour; in searching for some European tax harmonisation, it must be kept in mind that differences in tax rates are justified by equity as well as by efficiency considerations; the expansion of the EC's structural funds must not be conceived as a simple transfer of money but also as a way of reinforcing the competitiveness of peripheral regions and industrial regions in decline . . .

All these show the complexity of 'the economics of the Single European Act'. The completion of the internal market has to be achieved in a context of imperfect competition and under second-best conditions; its objective has profound implications for the allocation of resources, the distribution of gains and the stability of the whole economy; and its means must combine a general process of deregulation with forms of overall regulation constrained by the principle of 'subsidiarity'. One virtue of this volume is to demonstrate not only the relevance of recently developed economic tools for understanding these issues, but also their limits. The European project is much more than the completion of a market. It is largely determined by broad considerations of international politics and requires a formidable effort to build up a new society.

Brussels
1989

Notes on the Contributors

Martin Chalkley is a lecturer in the Department of Economics at the University of Southampton.

John Driffill is a professor in the Department of Economics at Queen Mary and Westfield College, University of London.

Paul Geroski is an associate professor at the London Business School.

Alan Hamlin is a senior lecturer in the Department of Economics at the University of Southampton.

Philip Hardwick is Commercial Union professor of finance at Bournemouth Polytechnic.

Peter Holmes is a lecturer in the School of European Studies at the University of Sussex.

George McKenzie is a reader in the Department of Economics and director of the Centre for International Economics at the University of Southampton.

Paul Turner is a lecturer in the Department of Economics at the University of Leeds.

Alistair Ulph is a professor in the Department of Economics at the University of Southampton.

Anthony Venables is Eric Roll professor of economic policy in the Department of Economics at the University of Southampton.

1 Introduction

George McKenzie and
Anthony J. Venables

In December 1985, the member countries of the European Community signed the Single European Act, the first major revision since the Treaty of Rome established the Community in 1957. By July 1987 the Act had been ratified by the Parliaments of all EC member states and passed into law. Amongst other things, this legislation commits the European Community to the goal of 'progressively establishing the internal market over a period expiring on 31 December 1992' where 'the internal market shall comprise an area without internal frontiers in which the free movement of goods, persons, services and capital is ensured'. In order to achieve this goal the Single European Act further amends the Treaty of Rome by removing the requirement that member states agree unanimously on many of the measures associated with completion of the internal market; measures which 'have as their objective the establishment and functioning of the internal market', fiscal measures apart, can now be passed by the Council of Ministers on the basis of 'qualified majority voting'. This guarantees the single market programme some immunity from the possible obstructionism of individual member states and ensures that implementation of the programme will proceed in a relatively rapid manner.

The detailed measures through which it is intended to achieve completion of the internal market are a set of some 300 directives put forward by the European Commission and discussed in a White Paper published in January 1985. The measures proposed in the Directives can be classified under three headings: removal of physical barriers to trade, removal of technical barriers, and removal of fiscal barriers, as outlined in Table 1.1

The possible effects of the removal of these barriers has already been the subject of much research. Economic gains might be expected to arise from three sources. First, some of the barriers are directly costly: for example time is wasted in frontier delays. Removal of such barriers will lead to immediate direct cost savings. Second, removal of trade barriers will cause countries to further

Table 1.1   Classification of EC directives for the completion of the internal European market

1. The removal of physical barriers:
   (a) Those pertaining to the control of trade in goods;
   (b) Those pertaining to the movement of individuals.
2. The removal of technical barriers:
   (a) Those pertaining to the free movement of goods:
       – Standards policies;
       – Sectoral proposals relating to: (i) motor vehicles; (ii) tractors and agricultural machines; (iii) food law; (iv) pharmaceuticals and high-technology medicines;
         (v) chemical products; (vi) construction and construction products; (vii) other items;
   (b) Public procurement;
   (c) Free movement of labour and the professions;
   (d) The Common Market for services: (i) financial services (i.e banking, insurance and securities markets); (ii) transport; and (iii) new technologies and services;
   (e) Capital movements within Europe;
   (f) Creation of suitable conditions for European cooperation;
   (g) The application of Community law.
3. The removal of fiscal barriers:
   (a) VAT;
   (b) Excise duties.

specialise in industries in which they have a comparative advantage, so bringing efficiency gains. Third, increased competition will lead to the survival of companies that are best able to exploit economies of scale in production. This will lead to cost and price reductions over and above those arising from comparative advantage. The 1992 directives would thus seem to be in the spirit of in the philosophy of Adam Smith who argued that competition and free trade would enable everyone to become better off.

A series of research studies undertaken for the European Commission attempts to quantify some of these effects, and the results of these studies are summarised in considerable detail in Commission of the European Communities (1988). The most optimistic calculations are reported in Table 1.2. Here the gains are divided into four categories. First it is seen that the gains associated with the removal of trade barriers are relatively small compared to the gains from the removal of restrictions affecting production. Second there are estimated to be substantial gains in terms of scale economies. In addition, the resulting increases in competition are likely to reduce

Table 1.2 Estimates of the economic gains associated with the completion of the internal European market (1985 prices)

Source	Billion ECU[1]	% GDP
1. Cost of barriers affecting trade only	9	0.3
2. Cost of barriers affecting all production	71	2.4
Total direct costs of barriers	80	2.7
3. Economies of scale from restructuring and increased competition	61	2.1
4. Competition effects on X-inefficiency and monopoly rents	46	1.6
Total market integration effects	107	3.7
Total Gains	187	6.4

1. One European Currency Unit (ECU) is worth approximately £0.655.

Source: Commission of the European Communities (1988), p. 157.

excessive monopoly profits and 'easy-life' behaviour on the part of European management. In other words this reduction in what is frequently referred to as X-inefficiency will lead to the survival of the fittest companies and financial institutions.

Of course, estimates of this type are subject to much uncertainty, and more research is needed if we are to gain a fuller understanding of the implications of the directives. The purpose of this volume is to take a step in this direction by presenting a set of essays which take a critical look at several of the issues posed by the directives. The essays were written in 1988 and early 1989, and range across the different aspects of economic life which are likely to be affected by completion of the market, covering trade and industry, the labour market, taxation, macroeconomics and financial services. Here is a brief overview.

Chapters 1 to 5 deal with trade and industrial aspects of 1992. Paul Geroski argues that the gains from restructuring and competition should not be overstated. Although there may be gains from economies of scale, the emergence of large companies marketing throughout Europe could lead to greater product standardisation and hence less consumer choice. Given the great diversity in preferences this effect could actually lead to a loss in satisfaction for many consumers. In addition, he claims that the post-1992 environment will not necessarily be conducive to technological innovation since it is the smaller companies which usually make the breakthroughs. One implication of Geroski's results is that public procurement policies should discriminate in favour of the smaller suppliers.

Peter Holmes raises a similar theme in his chapter on non-tariff barriers, the special product standards and border formalities that inhibit international trade within Europe by making it more costly. He argues that the European Commission estimates may be overstated. However, the projected gains could come about if there are widespread changes in corporate strategies and attitudes. If the publicity surrounding the lead-up to 1992 is effective, Holmes claims, then there will be a change in psychology. But this will only occur if the governments are committed to implementation. Any questioning of objectives such as has frequently been done by members of the British government is bound to create an environment of uncertainty and create a situation where the UK economy finds itself in a weaker competitive position *vis-à-vis* its committed European trading partners.

Tony Venables examines the gains from trade. One of the fundamental conjectures of the Commission is that the 1992 Directives will increase competition and lead to a reduction in monopoly positions that companies may have enjoyed in protected national markets. Venables, however, calls attention to the fact that companies with strong market power may still be able to exploit their position by acting in a discriminatory fashion in national markets. As a result the gains presented in Table 1.2 could be significantly eroded. An important policy implication emerges. European anti-trust policy must be rigorously applied if monopolies which enjoy economies of scale are not to further exploit their power and to discriminate in ways which actually lead to divergences in prices between markets rather than the anticipated narrowing.

In Chapter 4, Alan Hamlin and Alistair Ulph discuss tax harmonisation. They start from first principles by identifying the conditions for an optimal European tax structure. They argue that because consumer preferences are so different between European Community members it is unlikely that an identical tax structure across all countries is desirable. Indeed they argue that if taxes were harmonised then a system of international transfer payments would need to be devised to ensure that the countries which lose as a result of the harmonisation are compensated by the gainers.

Labour market issues are discussed by Martin Chalkley in Chapter 5. He provides us with empirical evidence which suggests that the completion of the internal European market will reduce unemployment in the UK. However, because labour is relatively immobile in this country it is possible that regional disparities could develop along the lines currently being experienced: unemployment in the North and Midlands and skill shortages in the South. Much of British management is currently taking these shortages as given. However, if Britain is to maintain and improve its competitive position then it must be the case that skill levels are improved. This will require greater government assistance to the education sector at all levels, from the training of electronics technicians to improving the awareness of corporate management to the opportunities that are available to them in the 1990s and beyond.

As can be seen from Table 1.1 the emphasis of the 1992 Directives is clearly on improving the efficiency of the European productive sector by removing barriers to trade and competition. However, there are also developments which will affect competition in the financial sector and in turn influence the manner in which monetary and government expenditure policies are implemented. These issues are discussed in Chapters 6 to 8. In his chapter Phillip Hardwick outlines the gains that are likely to occur as a result of greater competition in banking, securities markets and insurance. He notes that the gains forecast in a study prepared for the European Commission are quite substantial. However, he raises a caveat similar to that made by Venables, namely that the existence of imperfect competition in financial markets may reduce the potential gains.

Although it was not an issue explicitly addressed when the EC member states signed the Single Act, the unrestricted mobility of funds between member states implied by the elimination of capital controls has important implications for the execution of macroeconomic policies. As John Driffill and Paul Turner and George McKenzie point out in their respective chapters, integrated financial markets imply that national monetary policies will become relatively ineffective. For example, if the Bank of England raised interest rates in order to slow down monetary growth, funds would flow in from abroad and thereby render the policy ineffective. Driffill and Turner suggest that greater policy coordination within the European Monetary System will be required. However, McKenzie argues that even this may not be sufficient. The uncertainty of possible future exchange realignments between European currencies increases actual and perceived costs of international transactions. Therefore he argues that full monetary union including the use of a common currency is necessary if all the potential benefits of a single European market are to be achieved. These issues are recognised. In June 1988, the European Council noted that 'in adopting the Single Act, the Member States of the community confirmed the objective of progressive realisation of economic and monetary union'. To that end a committee under the chairmanship of Jacques Delors was established. This committee has now reported. Amongst its many recommendations is the creation of a European System of Central Banks which would replace existing national monetary authorities. The obvious cost of this proposal to each country is loss of sovereignty. However, this loss may actually be irrelevant anyway if monetary policy is ineffective at a national level and if the gains from freer trade and competition are thought to be desirable.

Further Reading

Much has been and will continue to be written about the economic effects of the Single European Act and the associated Directives. Two volumes are essential background reading for anyone interested in the lead-up to 1992: Cecchini (1988) and Commission of the European Communities (1988).

References

Cecchini, P. (1988) *The European Challenge: 1992*, Gower, London.
Commission of the European Communities (March 1988) 'The Economics of 1992', *European Economy*. Special edition, 35, pp. 1–222.

2 1992 and European Industrial Structure

P.A. Geroski

2.1 INTRODUCTION

It is not difficult to understand why a large number of people appear to get rather excited by the mere mention of 1992. Europe, it is widely agreed, has (and has, for too long, had) an industrial performance problem, and the gamut of policies associated with 1992 are seen as a possible solution to a pressing concern. They are, moreover, a solution that is consistent with the aspirations embodied in the 1957 Treaty of Rome, and, indeed, are seen by many as the last step in what has been a long path of realisation. Better still, they are easy to understand and are apparently easy to implement (in principle at least). Finally, their spirit is wholly in keeping with the adulation of free market processes which currently passes for policy thinking in many European capitals, and, yet, despite this, both the plain man and the industrial policy enthusiast can agree that the 1992 policies are, on the whole, both reasonable and sensible. For a Europe that feels badly in need of a success, 1992 has all the promise of the first day of spring.

The basic reasoning underlying the 1992 solution starts with the observation that the internal Community market is fragmented into a series of national (and sometimes regional) markets, each surrounded by a series of trade barriers. Firms which operate in the various nation states are insulated from the forces of competition, and their quest to achieve the benefits of scale is restricted by the relatively limited size of their protected home markets. For both reasons, then, they are inefficient, and are likely to be overwhelmed by their Japanese and American rivals in any kind of open competitive contest. Removing the various trade barriers that inhibit the integration of the various national markets into one large, unified Community market is the obvious solution to this problem, and this, in a nutshell, is what the 1992 policy programme proposes to do. The direct benefits are likely to manifest themselves in a reduction in both

7

the average level and the intra-Community dispersion of prices for particular goods. Longer run, but, it is thought, more substantial are the benefits which will emerge indirectly from the restructuring of industry that the removal of trade barriers will, it is hoped, induce. Freed from the restriction of narrow national markets, European enterprises will be able to grow and specialise, reaping all the advantages that large-scale operations are thought to bring. The increase in competition that attends the removal of trade barriers will, naturally, stimulate this drive towards efficiency, and, it is hoped, also encourage innovation. Although harder to describe and measure, these indirect benefits are, it is argued, the real prize, and will ultimately lead to a European industrial structure capable of holding its own in the highly competitive global market-place.

To evaluate the claims underlying this vision, one must start by asking whether Europe is, in fact, badly fragmented. This question has recently been the subject of a major research project undertaken by the EC Commission and, in section 2.2, we shall critically examine the results that have emerged from that work. If the internal Community market is indeed fragmented, the next question to ask is whether it can be unified, and the extent to which the 1992 policy programme will succeed in so doing. This is the subject of section 2.3. Supposing that unification is possible, the final question to be asked is what will happen when it has been achieved. There are, in fact, several possible consequences for Europe's industrial structure of implementing the 1992 programme, some more desirable than others. Assessing which of these is most likely depends not only on whether there are substantial advantages to size, but also on the types of policies which accompany the 1992 programme. Several scenarios are possible, and these are discussed in section 2.4. Our concluding remarks in section 2.5 return to the question of whether 1992 will prove to be the grand apocalypse that some have promised it will be.

2.2   IS EUROPE FRAGMENTED?

In 1987, the population of the European Community was about 323 million, nearly a third larger than the US and two and a half times the size of Japan. The question at issue is whether Europe really constitutes as large a market as this comparison implies, or whether it is merely twelve national markets situated in close geographical proximity.

The answer to this question hinges on how freely goods and services cross national borders. There are a variety of obstacles which inhibit trade flows between the member states, some natural and some strategically erected by national governments to protect their own domestic industrial interests. Most of these strategic obstacles take the form of absolute cost advantages enjoyed by domestic firms *vis-à-vis* firms in other member countries, and the wedge that they create between the cost of imports and of domestically produced goods creates scope for domestic firms to exercise some degree of market power. In particular, if c_f are the costs incurred by foreign firms and c_d are the costs incurred by domestic firms, then $(c_f - c_d)/c_d$ is the percentage mark-up over costs that domestic firms can charge without attracting competitive entry from firms in other member countries. Roughly speaking, this mark-up can be thought of as a rate of return on sales which is sustainable in perpetuity in the face of entry, and, as such, it is a natural measure of market power. $(c_f - c_d)/c_d$ gives both a measure of the degree of market power created by fragmentation, as well as a measure of the gains to be realised by removing the various obstacles to trade.

Although $(c_f - c_d)/c_d$ is a natural way to measure the height of barriers to trade, it can, in some ways, be slightly misleading. There are a variety of factors which can drive a wedge between c_d and c_f, but the ones that are of most importance in the current context are those that are avoidable, those which yield little benefit and can be costlessly removed. Technical regulations designed to ensure that certain standards of safety are met may yield a benefit which more than compensates for their effects on price; transport costs, by contrast, benefit no one but cannot be costlessly removed. Further, if scale economies exist, then the removal of trade obstacles can give rise to further, possibly more profound gains as restructuring occurs to exploit the advantages of scale, gains that a measure like $(c_f - c_d)/c_d$ does not fully capture.

Brushing these problems aside and taking $(c_f - c_d)/c_d$ to be a rough and ready measure of the height of barriers to entry still leaves one with the problem of interpreting the numbers that one gets by using it. In particular, it is important to ask: 'how high is high?' Bain (1956) argued that barriers were 'high' if they enabled incumbents to raise prices 10 per cent above costs persistently without attracting entry; 'substantial' and 'moderate to low' barriers would support prices 7 per cent and not more than 4 per cent above costs respectively (p. 170). Although an enormous amount of work has been done in identifying the sources of barriers to entry, relatively few quantitative estimates of the overall height of barriers to entry exist. However, some work of relevance has been reported by Geroski (1988a) and Fairburn and Geroski (1988), who studied entry by foreign and domestic firms into UK three digit industries in the 1970s and early 1980s respectively. Both studies found that, on average, incumbents could sustain price-cost margins of about 17 per cent in the face of entry, and both found that the height of barriers facing foreign and domestic firms was, on average across all manufacturing industries, about the same. Although both the sources and overall height of barriers were not the same for foreign and domestic firms industry by industry, the two were positively correlated across industries. These numbers suggest two points worth keeping in mind when evaluating the obstacles which are thought to have fragmented the internal Community market. First, domestic and foreign based entry do not appear to be perfect substitutes (see also Geroski, 1988b), a result which suggests that removing obstacles to intra-Community trade will not necessarily make all markets competitive. Second, mark-ups of the order of (say) 5 per cent attributed to trade obstacles are rather modest compared to the kinds of barrier that purely domestic entrants appear to face. If one combines estimates of trade obstacles of (say) 5 per cent with the numbers referred to above, the obvious conclusion to draw is that, fragmented or not, the obstacles to movements between member nations are certainly no greater than those which inhibit intersectoral mobility within nation states. Although rigidities within national economies could be construed as a European problem, it is less than clear that it needs a European solution.

The Commission has argued that there are a range of obstacles to trade which are avoidable, and these might usefully be grouped under three headings: customs procedures, technical regulations, and public procurement practices. Let us consider each in turn.

Customs procedures have arisen to handle problems of tax adjustment arising from national differences in VAT, to deal with issues arising from health and transport regulations, and to ensure compliance with bilateral trade quota regimes. The costs that they create reveal themselves in paper mountains, long waiting times at border crossings, and personnel devoted to the exciting and deeply satisfying task of filling out forms. Based on a survey of about 470 firms in six member countries, the Commission estimated that the major component of costs was administrative costs, totalling about 7.5 billion

ECU, or 1.5 per cent of the value of internal trade. The cost of frontier delays and the cost to public authorities of creating them add between 1 and 2 billion further ECU to this total (EC, 1988, p. 48). However, a much larger-scale survey of business perceptions of trade obstacles found that frontier costs are thought to be somewhat less important than those associated with technical standards (EC, 1988, p. 48). They were, however, ranked as most important in textiles, footwear and clothing, paper, mineral oil refining, rubber products, precision engineering and food (EC, 1988, p. 46). More interesting were the observations that costs per consignment could be as much as 30–40 per cent higher for small firms (less than 250 employees), and that costs associated with customs procedures were particularly (and possibly unbelievably) high for goods passing in and out of Italy; Belgium maintained the most open frontier.

Technical regulations, standards and testing/certification procedures govern the specifications of goods which can be sold in the various national markets. Some of these are safety regulations, and some are concerned with health. There are tens of thousands of these regulations, all detailed, complex and written in a turgid legalese which bares little resemblance to any language spoken in the Community. They appear to be particularly prevalent in electrical and mechanical engineering, pharmaceuticals, food and precision and medical equipment (EC, 1988, p. 51). The Commission was unable to put an overall figure on the height of barriers that these obstacles create, but a survey of 20,000 enterprises in the 12 member countries did rank these barriers as being the most important of all (EC, 1988, p. 44). Industrialists in plastic, non-metal mineral products, chemicals, metal articles, mechanical engineering and transport all ranked them as the most important set of obstacles that they faced (EC, 1988, p. 46). They were also perceived to be more important by small rather than large firms (EC, 1988, p. 47). Examples such as pasta purity laws in Italy, wood-working machines entering France, and automatic telephone exchanges yielded estimates of trade obstacles around the 10 per cent region (EC, 1988, p. 53), although it must be said that not all of these extra costs are avoidable.

Public procurement policies in the various member states tend to systematically favour domestic over foreign suppliers. They are often used to build up and sustain 'national champions', and are often justified by various types of 'infant industry' arguments. Although most obvious (and most conspicuously wasteful) in the area of defence spending, the fact is that public procurement often plays a major role early in the lifecycle of industries that most of us agree are 'winners'. The Commission explored 40 goods frequently purchased by public sector bodies, and, comparing actual to minimum Community prices (correcting for trade costs), deduced that open tendering might save 3 billion ECU. They then argued that open tendering would lead to a major restructuring of the industries concerned and to an increase in competition, contributing perhaps another 8 billion ECU in savings. Including defence spending produces a total (direct plus those to be realised largely in the medium and long run) saving of about 0.6 per cent of Community GDP. It is worth stressing that the major gains to liberalising public procurement policies are thought to result from the restructuring of production and the reduction in excess capacity that competition and a larger internal market are expected to induce. In industrial boilers, for example, restructuring is thought likely to yield cost savings of 20 per cent; turbine generators, locomotives and telephone hand sets promise 12, 20 and 30–40 per cent savings respectively (EC, 1988, p. 60).

As we have seen, it is likely that removing the various obstacles to intra-Community trade will have quite different effects in different industries, and it is worth looking at several industries in detail to get a feel for what is involved, and what might happen. In food processing, for example, there are a variety of restrictions on content, labelling and packaging, as well as various specific prohibitions on certain inputs on products (EC, 1988, pp. 66–9). The benefit to removing these is thought to be about 1–2 per cent of turnover, and is concentrated in about seven products: beer, pasta, aspartame, vegetable fats in chocolate, vegetable fats in ice cream, saccharine and bans on using plastic containers for mineral water and non-alcoholic beverages (EC, 1988, pp. 67–8). Typical of these regulations is that in Italy prohibiting the use of common (as opposed to durum) wheat in pasta. The removal of these is thought likely to generate savings of between 35 million and 100 million ECU per year. Purity standards for beer in Germany are cited as a typical example of how such obstacles lead to inefficient production, with too many producers (75 per cent of all Community brewers apparently) crowded into an over-protected market. Cost savings of 3–7 per cent of beer value added are anticipated from a restructuring of the industry into a smaller number of large producers. In telecommunications, the major issues are procurement policies and technical standards (EC, 1988, pp. 77–8), with national governments actively supporting and discriminating in favour of their national champions. The gains from standardising technical specifications are thought to be in the region of 0.58–1.1 billion ECU, while those resulting from a more competitive procurement regime are thought to be in the range 2.2–3.7 billion ECU, a total of 17–27 per cent of the 1986 value of the telecommunications market. Building products suffer from technical specifications which impede trade (EC, 1988, pp. 76–7), while pharmaceuticals suffer particularly from delays induced by registration requirements (EC, 1988, pp. 69–71). By contrast little effect is anticipated in automobiles. Various technical advances in production, thought likely to amount to savings of 5 per cent of unit cost, will probably be realised whether or not 1992 occurs (EC, 1988, p. 73). Similarly, little saving is expected in textiles and clothing (EC, 1988, pp. 74–6).

What sectors are currently most afflicted with trade obstacles, and thus eventually most likely to be affected by 1992 policies? The evidence is sufficiently thin to make it difficult to tell for sure, but one senses that procurement practices and technical regulations are the major sources of obstacles. This, in turn, suggests that energy (which accounts for 16.3 per cent of total public purchasing in the community), electrical goods (4.6 per cent), transport (10.1 per cent), chemicals (3.2 per cent), machinery (4.6 per cent), construction (28.6 per cent) and various services (21.8 per cent) on the one hand (EC, 1988, p. 55), and engineering, pharmaceuticals, food and precision and medical equipment on the other (EC, 1988, p. 51) will be the most affected (if at all). This list turns out to include a number of dynamic, high technology, high growth sectors where Community firms have, apparently, been losing external and internal market shares. Office machinery, data processing, precision instruments, electrical goods and electronics are all thought to be areas where '. . . fragmentation of the Community constitutes a serious handicap . . .' (EC, 1988, p. 25). This correlation between sectors where intra-Community trade is fragmented and sectors whose international performance is poor is, in many ways, the link which is thought to validate the vision underlying the 1992 programme. 'The fragmentation of Community industry constitutes a serious handicap in these industrial markets. In these high tech sectors, the critical mass for R&D is considerable . . . Furthermore, economies of scale play a vital role in these industries . . .' (EC, 1988, p. 25). The implication is that Euroenterprises and Euroconsortia are the solution to the performance problem, and the suggestion is that these will emerge when the European market is unified.

There are three important features of the estimates of barriers to trade that we have reviewed thus far which are worth further comment. First, it seems reasonable to think that most of the gains to 1992 will be concentrated in a few sectors (and probably mainly in a few industries within each sector). The few sectors that we have mentioned as being potentially most affected may actually be virtually the only ones affected. In the main, it is firms and industries that are smothered by technical or health regulations, or which regularly supply the public sector, which seem likely to be most affected. Second, it appears that only a small proportion of the total benefits to flow from 1992 are directly associated with removing barriers. Rather more than half of the total savings of 5.8–6.4 per cent of Community GDP that are claimed to be within reach are associated with restructuring and competition (EC, 1988, p. 155), and these will take 5–10 years to realise (EC, 1988, p. 156). Third, expressed in terms of mark-ups, the claimed savings are quite small. Five or 6 per cent mark-ups are hardly substantial, and numbers that small are probably not terribly robust to mismeasurement or to calculation errors. Certainly they do not compare to the kinds of mark-ups traditionally associated with high entry barriers, and one senses that a policy which reduces the entry barriers facing only one type of entrant is an incomplete policy no matter how you look at it. Still, a small percentage of a very large number is a large number, and 5.8–6.4 per cent of Community GDP adds up to 171–187 billion ECU, between 530 and 580 ECU per head of the 1987 Community population. The moral, then, is that the policies of 1992 will pay (if at all) not so much because the barriers to be removed are (on average) high, as because the size of the market over which the price effects will operate is large. A small percentage gain given to a lot of people is, in aggregate, a large absolute gain.

Another way to gain some perspective on the size of barriers which the 1992 programme is aimed at is to look at the extent of price dispersion across a number of countries. The rather modest size (as measured by the direct effects of removing them) of many of the barriers that the Commission identified suggests that the prices of a given good throughout the Community ought to be fairly similar. A barrier which drives a 5 per cent wedge between domestic and foreign costs of production is likely to create a price differential of the same order of magnitude. However, the evidence that exists on price dispersion clearly shows that prices vary enormously within the Community. Consumers of cars, white goods, clothing, pharmaceuticals and other goods will need little persuading of this. Car prices vary enormously between countries. In 1983, for example, prices in the UK were nearly 44 per cent higher (before and after taxes) than in Belgium; prices in the FRG were 23 per cent and 11 per cent higher, prices in France were 19 per cent and 25 per cent higher and those in Italy were 32 per cent and 29 per cent higher than in Belgium (Mertens and Ginsburgh, 1985). Washing machines also vary enormously in price across Europe, with France, Germany and Italy being the most expensive in the mass market, and Belgium the lowest in both mass and premium markets. A machine that cost £270 in the UK in 1986, for example, cost £362 in France, £292 in the FRG in 1985, £305 in Belgium in 1985, and £390 in Italy in 1987 (see Nicolaides and Baden-Fuller, 1987). In clothing, prices net of tax for (say) men's sporting outfits are 64 per cent higher in France than in the UK, 25 per cent higher in Italy, and 1 per cent lower in Germany. Woollen skirts are twice as expensive in Denmark as in the UK, but slightly cheaper still in Greece (Rossini, 1988). Pharmaceuticals prices, to take a final example, vary enormously, differing by as much as a factor of 10 across countries. Prices exclusive of taxes on average were 24 per cent higher in Germany than Ireland, 39 per cent higher in Ireland than Belgium, and 19 per cent higher in Belgium than in France in 1983 (EEC, 1988, pp. 69–70).

More broadly, the Commission examined prices for about 90-odd goods sold throughout the Community, and found that the standard deviation of price dispersion was about 27 per cent of average price, suggesting that a product which sells for (say) £1 in the UK is likely to be priced in the £1.25–£1.40 to £0.75–£0.60 range elsewhere (EC, 1988, p. 118). Of course, part of this observed dispersion is due to taxes (perhaps about a quarter according to Commission estimates) and the degree of dispersion is higher, it appears, in sectors where there are high non-tariff barriers (EC, 1988, pp. 121, 122). However, these barriers appear to be only a small part of the explanation of the high degree of observed price dispersion. In cars, for example, '. . . formal barriers to intra-Community trade . . . turn out to have a relatively marginal impact . . .' on price variation (EC, 1988, p. 74), much of which is sustained by the selective distribution system authorised by the Commission in 1985 (EC, 1988, p. 72). VAT rates on washing machines are virtually identical across countries, and the price differences that are created by VAT differences are more than dwarfed by differences in retail prices. Trade barriers in textiles are thought to affect unit costs by less than 1 per cent in general, but, since it is '. . . not so likely that potential reductions in production costs will be translated automatically into production prices' (EC, 1988, p. 75), it is hard to see how current trade barriers could be sustaining the price dispersion that we observe. Much the same applies in pharmaceuticals where ' . . . the direct costs associated with multiple registration are small' (EC, 1988, p. 70). The obvious implication is that there is something in addition to (and probably much more important than) trade barriers which drives a wedge between the prices of similar goods in different national markets. Although there may be some supply side factors responsible for this, one suspects that a large percentage of the variation in intra-Community prices reflect subtle differences in product specification that cater to local tastes, as well as monopolistic pricing to exploit differences in demand elasticities. In short, even if all barriers to trade were eliminated tomorrow, one would still expect a substantial amount of price dispersion to persist well past 1992, and perhaps in perpetuity.

Is Europe fragmented then? The answer to this question is almost certainly 'yes'. However, except in a relatively small number of industries, the reasons why this is the case may have a lot less to do with obstacles to trade than 1992 enthusiasts assert. Even the most relentlessly self-centred and parochial American tourist visiting Europe is regularly struck by the diversity of tastes, styles and cultures in Europe, and most are continually delighted by it. Similarly, many scholars have noted the thinness of supply and the high concentration of many markets in Europe, a situation which is not unrelated to the diversity of tastes. That such factors are an important component of the fragmentation of European markets is no surprise. What is, perhaps, something of a surprise is how thoroughly they appear to dominate the obstacles to trade that the 1992 programme proposes to dismantle.

2.3   CAN EUROPE BE UNIFIED?

The core of the 1992 programme is fairly easy to summarise. First, frontier controls and border checks will, it is hoped, be eliminated, and, to do this, it is necessary to eliminate the need for border tax adjustment, health and transport standards checking and the enforcement of various bilateral trade quotas (EC, 1988, pp. 44, 46). The major plank in this programme is undoubtedly the elimination of fiscal frontiers through the harmonisation of VAT and excise duties (EC, 1988, pp. 61–5). Second, a variety of policies will be directed at reducing differences in technical standards (EC, 1988, p. 50). A mutual recognition principle towards national regulations is proposed, to be complemented by attempts to harmonise national technical regulations, improve the functioning of European standardisation bodies and improve the flow of information regarding new standards and regulations. Finally, it is intended that public procurement should be opened up to Community-wide competition (EC, 1988, p. 54).

Supplementing these basic policies are a range of accompanying policies which are deemed to be necessary to ensure that the full benefits of the basic programme are realised (EC, 1988, pp. 138–40). Perhaps the most important of these is concerned with competition policy. Firms that grow large enough to exploit the advantages of size are likely to achieve a dominant position in the markets they operate in, and this may lead to a number of undesirable outcomes. Similarly, cooperative R&D projects – a development to be welcomed whenever individual firms find it difficult to achieve a critical R&D mass on their own – must not be allowed to extend to cooperation into other dimensions (like price setting). State aids and subsidies to promote national champions or to protect domestic producers must be carefully monitored, and credible sanctions must be devised and applied to those governments that unduly favour their own national firms and industries. Competition policy is, however, not the only policy which should accompany the 1992 programme. The specialisation that unifying the internal market may create may lead to an uneven distribution of gains and losses across countries. National industries may expand in some countries and contract or disappear in others, creating short- and medium-run adjustment problems. Some system of compensation between 'winners' and 'losers' is necessary lest national rivalries explode into major Community tensions. Finally, completing the internal market may lead to some rethinking of the common external policy, particularly in areas where European enterprises emerge strong and ready to face open competition in global markets.

There seems to be a good deal of sense in proposals to simplify customs procedures and, even if VAT harmonisation proves impossible to implement, it ought to be possible to simplify the procedures governing border tax adjustments. Although the benefits of such policies are not, perhaps, likely to be very large, the costs involved are pretty much avoidable. There is also no doubt that opening up procurement procedures is a good idea, and it is reasonable to think that the potential for big gains exist in the areas like telecommunications. However, while it is possible to see big potential gains to liberalising procurement, it is hard to believe that much more than a slow, stumbling progress will actually be made. Many national governments see procurement as a method of developing and nurturing industries which are strategically important. It is easy to curse the apparently myopic nationalism that underlies such views, but the fact is that sectors like electronics spawn a wide range of offshoot activities, and any member state which does not maintain a substantial presence in the sector is likely to lose out on all the spin-offs. Although free trade may benefit the Community as a whole, individual countries will always be able to improve their own position with carefully placed restrictions, and procurement policies seem likely to be the area where such departures are most likely to be observed. The arguments put forward for eliminating health and technical standards are perhaps the weakest of all. Maintaining the durum wheat content of pasta or banning the use of plastic containers for mineral water are, no doubt, egregious examples of abuse. However, the use of technical and health standards in general is a practice solidly based on a laudable desire to protect both consumers and honest manufacturers from the predations of hit-and-run entrants who capitalise on information asymmetries. There is no doubt that establishing Europe-wide standards is a step in the right direction, but it is hard to believe that legitimate differences in national preferences will simply disappear in the process. Building practices and products are, for example, strongly affected by cultural and climatic conditions, and have long since been internalised into the working procedures of builders and building materials suppliers (EC, 1988, pp. 76–7). Practices appropriate to Greece will not do for the UK or Denmark, and it is not obvious that harmonisation of many of them has any merit at all. That is, technical standards to create obstacles to trade, but it is not obvious that they are avoidable. Finally, it is hard to dispute the need for a strong and vigorous competition (and regulatory) policy, particularly in those sectors where large firms exploiting scale economies operate. Indeed, of all the proposals in the 1992 programme, this seems to be the most sensible and the most desirable. What is more, its appeal does not hinge on any of the claims about market fragmentation or the advantages to size that sustain the rest of the 1992 programme.

Sensible as these 1992 policies are, the question of whether they will really unify Europe remains open. The promise of 1992 is that of large gains from restructuring European enterprise on a European scale, but this requires that trade barriers be eliminated, and tastes harmonised. Mass production brings efficiency gains by standardising products and then producing them in volume; however, this, in turn, carries a cost borne by consumers who can no longer consume the exact combination of characteristics that they wish to. If consumer's tastes are similar, then no major problems arise; if, however, they are diverse, then mass producers will always lose out to smaller, customised niche producers. In this latter case, no gains to a large-scale rationalisation of production will emerge, and fragmented market structures will remain fragmented. The point is of major importance since it is by no means clear that obstacles to trade are the main reason why few European firms operate on a truly European scale. The ability to produce Eurogoods cheaply by producing them in large quantities is of precious little value if no one wants to consume them; efficiency is hardly worth the effort if too much variety is sacrificed to achieve it.

Of course, everything has its price, and even those who dislike fizzy soft drinks will chose to drink coke rather than mineral water if it is cheap enough. The real question, then, is whether the advantages of large-scale production consequent on standardisation are large enough to compensate for the potential horrors of a few Eurofirms producing Eurogoods on a truly European scale. The basic flaw in the 1992 vision is that they are not, and this, in turn, means that the real benefit of the 1992 programme is that it will extend the diversity that exists across Europe into each of the individual national markets. Attempts to standardise goods across markets will simply squander the potential that Europe has before it.

2.4   1992 AND ALL THAT

The major prop upon which the 1992 vision rests is a belief in the pervasiveness of scale economies. Large size is often thought to bring competitive strength, and scale economies are perhaps the most easily understood and most widely accepted rationale for this view. The question, as always, is 'how large is large?' If production at less than minimum efficient scales is impossible (or is prohibitively expensive), then the larger minimum efficient scale is as a proportion of market size, the smaller is the number of firms that can compete in a homogeneous goods market. If, for example, minimum efficient scale were 5 per cent of the total market, then a maximum of 20 firms would be viable; if efficient scale were 10 per cent of the market, then at most 10 would be viable. Although it is hard to be sure, one feels that the kind of restructuring that the Commission anticipates and the size of the expected benefits that they hope to reap thereby requires the existence of minimum efficient scale well in excess of 10–15 per cent. Numbers of this magnitude will result in perhaps two to five major Eurofirms producing Eurogoods in most markets, with another ten to fifteen producing more differentiated variants which sell Europe-wide, although perhaps on a smaller scale and unevenly distributed across nations. The two to five majors will, in some sense, represent 'European champions', and, taking advantage of the scale economies that a market of 323 million consumers permit, these champions should more than hold their own globally.

The major problem with this vision of the future is that the evidence presented by the Commission on the size of scale economies hardly supports the hopes that rest on it. There are a variety of ways to measure scale economies (e.g. see the discussion in Scherer (1980), Chapter 4), and the Commission very sensibly relied on those (so called 'engineering estimates') which, as it were, design plants from scratch using the best, most up-to-date technology. Their main advantage is that they enable us to measure the potential levels that can be achieved using best-practice technology in a way which enables one to ascertain whether actual plant and production practices measure up. These types of estimates are, naturally, rather difficult to construct, and the evidence amassed by the Commission takes the form of a range of estimates that have been made over the last decade or so. Most of the industries surveyed (89 per cent of them) exhibited levels of minimum efficient scale less than 10 per cent of the Community market, and three quarters were less than 5 per cent (EC, 1988, p. 110). Further, the penalty to sub-minimum efficient scale production was found to be fairly modest in most sectors, leading one to suspect that most markets could sustain at least twenty efficient producers, and often considerably more. The only sectors in which one could sense real potential gains from scale (and substantial penalties to sub-efficient scale production) were aircrafts, chemicals, electric motors and paper (EC, 1988, p. 110).

In fact, it is almost certain that numbers like this overstate the advantages to scale. Most of the studies from which these numbers were culled contain a major sample selection bias in that they focused on industries that were thought likely to exhibit major scale economies. They are, therefore, quite likely to overstate the incidence and importance of scale economies in the total population of industries. It is also the case that this type of estimate of scale economies overstates the benefits likely to be realised in practice, largely because they focus on what is technologically possible without considering organisational or managerial constraints. It is one thing to build a gigantic plant when technology dictates large size; it is another thing altogether to manage a plant that large. The fact is that large plants are difficult to manage. They are noticeably more strike prone than smaller establishments (e.g. Prais, 1978), and the sour industrial relations climate that they frequently create generally forces managers to pay higher wages to attract workers. These managerial constraints on managing large plants go some way towards explaining why comparative productivity studies generally fail to find plant size to be an important factor in explaining productivity differences between countries (e.g. see the case studies discussed in Prais, (1981)). Indeed, UK performance appears to be inferior in those sectors where its plants are largest, particularly because of the poor performance of the large plants in those sectors (Caves and Davies, 1987, pp. 68). Indeed, the comparative disadvantage of large firms has become clear over the last few years in the increasingly evident shift towards small-scale production (e.g Oulton, 1987). All of this ought to be familiar to the common man. The distribution of plant sizes that one observes in virtually every industry is enormous, even in industries where scale is thought to be important, and many mergers which are designed to exploit scale economies (or other sources of synergy) fail, leaving bloated and inefficient enterprises in their wake (for a careful study, see Cowling *et al.* (1980)). It is inconceivable that such an enormous range of plant sizes would exist were scale economies large and the penalty to sub-optimal production great. Similarly, even if there were big advantages to large-scale establishments and enterprises, the high failure rate of mergers indicates that only a relatively small number of managers can handle the organisational problems which hinder their realisation.

The bottom line, then, is that the evidence presented on scale economies is rather underwhelming, particularly when one acknowledges that the methods and types of estimates used tend to exaggerate the potential gains of large size. That there are, in general, few good reasons to encourage the growth of large-scale enterprises producing standardised goods in large establishments does not, of course, mean that such a strategy is all bad. However, there are at least three further reasons why one might regard such a strategy with a great deal of suspicion. First, the gains to scale, such as they are, must be sufficiently large to overcome the costs to consumers of a reduced variety of choice, and all the evidence suggests that the desire for differentiation – for distinctive variety, for personalised services and so on – increases with affluence (see, for example, the stimulating argument by Hirsch (1977)). The demand for variety – particularly when there are frequent changes in consumer preferences for specific product characteristics – requires a production structure geared to flexibility and customised production, characteristics which are almost certainly sacrificed in a drive for large–scale specialisation in the production of standardised goods (on the trade-off involved between efficiency and flexibility, see Carlsson (1989)). Second, whatever the size of scale economies, they are unlikely to be realised if competitive pressures are not strong. There is little to be gained by creating giant firms to exploit scale economies if doing so destroys the competitive pressures that are necessary to induce firms to achieve the potential cost savings available. Third, much more striking than the modest potential for cost reduction through removing trade barriers identified by the Commission is the enormous degree of price dispersion that exists across the national markets in Europe, and the fact is that there is little evidence to suggest that removing trade barriers will have much more impact on it. Although much of this price variation is due to product differentiation, much also represents the effects of monopoly power. Encouraging the growth of large Eurofirms whose activities span a number of markets simultaneously will do nothing to reduce price discrimination, and is, in fact, likely to worsen the problem. When set against what are, in general, pretty modest looking gains, these three disadvantages suggest that there is a lot to be said against a policy of encouraging the growth of Eurofirms producing Eurogoods.

Thus, the industrial structure which the Commission thinks likely to emerge from the 1992 policies is, in fact, unlikely to occur without encouragement from policy-makers willing to promote or bless mergers based on the most ephemeral and extravagant of claims. Except in a few sectors, scale economies are not very large, and, faced with the fact of major diversities in consumption patterns within Europe, are unlikely to be strong enough to create genuine market pressures which encourage the emergence of more than a few

Eurofirms producing Eurogoods. Indeed, since many of the obstacles to trade outside telecommunications, defence and a few other sectors appear to be fairly small, the fact that Eurogoods have not yet appeared in most markets can be taken as a sure sign that they are unlikely to do so in the absence of conscious policy intervention. What is most important in the 1992 programme is the accompanying stress on a vigorous pro-competition policy. Many of the gains to be had from restructuring European industry can only be realised if competition remains vigorous, and, indeed, it is probably the case that virtually all of them can be realised just by stimulating competition. The importance of competition policy derives as much from the intrinsic gains that it promises as from the fact that it will protect Europe from those who seriously believe that Eurofirms producing Eurogoods are an answer to any problem that Europe faces. Europe post-1992 ought to display a diversity in output reflecting its rich diversity in culture, with medium-scale enterprises producing different types of goods in moderately competitive markets and shipping them throughout the Community (and, perhaps, the world) to the benefit of an increasingly affluent and discriminating group of consumers with diverse tastes. This is probably what will happen if the official enthusiasm for 1992 goes no further than dismantling trade barriers and pursuing a vigorous competition policy. Whether we will be lucky enough to achieve this remains an open question.

2.5 CONCLUSION

The 1992 programme has been the subject of an extraordinary amount of PR hype, most of which has involved exaggerating the benefits of the 1992 policies and neglecting their costs. The fact of the matter is that there are at least some good reasons to maintain national technical standards and to use procurement procedures to encourage 'infant industries', and there are also good reasons to dread the arrival of large-scale European enterprises peddling standardised goods throughout Europe in conditions of rather imperfect competition. This is, of course, not to say that there will be no gains to the 1992 programme. Eliminating pointless border crossing costs, protectionist specifications of standards and unnecessarily protectionist procurement policies are a good idea. They may lead to benefits in some sectors, and they will almost certainly make it easier for small national firms to compete in Europe. They will also bring benefits simply by reminding national businessmen that a European market exists and ought to be explored. Accompanied by a vigourous anti-trust policy, they may well produce a hard, lean and dynamically efficient European industrial sector ready to propel us into the twenty-first century. The bottom line, however, is that 1992 is already happening and will continue to do so long after 1992 has turned into 1993. As long as no one makes the mistake of thinking that 1992 portends a major restructuring which ought to be encouraged, there seems to be no harm in thinking that it is a date to look forward to.

References

Abernathy, W. *et al.* (1983) *Industrial Renaissance*, Basic Books, New York.
Bain, J. (1956) *Barriers to New Competition*, Harvard University Press, Cambridge, Mass.
Carlsson, B. (1989) 'Flexibility and the theory of the firm', forthcoming in the *International Journal of Industrial Organisation*.
Caves, R. and Davies, S. (1987) *Britain's Productivity Gap*, Cambridge University Press.
Cecchini, P. (1988) *The European Challenge*, Wildwood House, Aldershot.
Cowling, K. *et al.* (1980) *Mergers and Economic Performance*, Cambridge University Press.
Commission of the European Communities, (March 1988) 'The Economics of 1992', *European Economy*, special edition, 35, pp. 1–222.
Fairburn, J. and Geroski, P. (1988) *Domestic and Foreign Entry in the UK, 1983–1984*, mimeo, London Business School.
Geroski, P. (1988a) *The Effect of Entry on Profit Margins in the Short and Long Run*, mimeo, London Business School.
Geroski, P. (1988b) *The Interaction Between Domestic and Foreign Based Entrants*, mimeo, London Business School.
Helpman, E. and Krugman, P. (1986), *Market Structure and Foreign Trade*, MIT Press, Cambridge, Mass.
Hirsch, F. (1977), *Social Limits to Growth*, Routledge & Kegan Paul, London.
Jacquemin, A. and Sapir, A. (1988) 'European or world integration?', *Westwirtschaftliches Archiv*, Vol. 124, pp. 127–39.
Lancaster, K. (1979) *Variety, Equity and Efficiency*, Basil Blackwell, Oxford.
Mertens, Y. and Ginsburgh, V. (1985) 'Product differentiation and price discrimination in the European Community: The case of automobiles', *Journal of Industrial Economics*, Vol. 34, pp. 151–66.
Nicolaides, P. and Baden-Fuller, C. (1987) *Price Discrimination and Product Differentiation in the European Domestic Appliance Market*, mimeo, London Business School.
Oulton, N. (August 1987) 'Plant closures and the productivity miracle in manufacturing', *National Institute Economic Review*, pp. 53–9.

Padoa-Schioppa, T. (1987) *Efficiency, Stability and Equity*. European Commission, Brussels.

Prais, S. (1981) *Productivity and Industrial Structure*, Cambridge University Press.

Rossini, G. (1988) *Price Discrimination in the European Clothing Sector*, mimeo, University of Bologna.

Scherer, F.M. (1980) *Industrial Market Structure and Economic Performance*, Houghton Mifflin Boston.

3 Non-Tariff Barriers

Peter Holmes

3.1 INTRODUCTION

Reviewing the nature of the existing non-tariff barriers (NTBs) we find that with a few significant exceptions their direct cost to firms is really quite modest. EC experts estimate that frontier controls and administrative barriers to trade impose a burden of 0.2–0.3 per cent of EC GDP; but the EC market is distinctly fragmented and benefits of up to 5–6 per cent of GDP from full integration have been estimated. The impact of NTBs comes from the interplay between them and the actions by business and government to restrain competition. Eliminating the costs of non-harmonised standards and of border formalities will not necessarily produce the full 'dynamic' gains that the Commission hopes for. This will depend on a change in corporate strategy and mentality. The EC Commission appears to recognise this, and the 1992 exercise seeks to mould business expectations about the shape of Europe's economy in the 1990s. By itself the 1992 programme could not generate the changes in business attitudes needed to implement it, but there is a chance that the psychological component of the 'game' will succeed, provided governments appear resolutely pre-committed to implementation.

3.2 TARIFF AND NON-TARIFF BARRIERS: WHAT ARE THEY?

The heart of the 1992 programme is the removal of all 'non-tariff barriers' within the European Community. Tariffs or customs duties are taxes on goods when they cross frontiers. Non-tariff barriers are harder to define, but essentially consist of any deliberate measure which makes imported goods costlier or harder to obtain than equivalent home produced goods. ('Natural' barriers, e.g. distance, are not NTBs.)

There are four broad categories of non-tariff barriers in international trade:

(a) *Administrative or financial costs imposed on goods crossing borders*. Import licensing for Intra-EC trade in EC-produced goods was abolished in 1969, but paperwork may still be required (e.g. for circulation of non-EC produced goods restricted by regulation). Internal tax systems may well indirectly discriminate against categories of goods likely to be imports.

(b) *Differences in technical standards, regulations and certification procedures* may directly or indirectly discriminate against foreign goods sold within a country.

(c) *Nationalistic industrial policy measures* exist, notably restrictions on public sector purchases, and other promotional measures such as subsidies.

(d) *Monopolistic and cartellistic practices* by private business may involve lobbying for government measures to restrain competition.

In 1947 the General Agreement on Tariffs and Trade (GATT) froze the existing tariff levels of its signatories, and sought the 'general elimination of quantitative restrictions on trade' (Art. XI), which then mostly meant import licensing procedures. The Treaty of Rome, in 1957, decreed the total abolition between member states of the six members of the original European Economic Community of both customs tariffs and all 'quantitative restrictions and measures having equivalent effect' (Articles 13 and 30). The EC did succeed in abolishing internal industrial goods tariffs by 1969. (The Common Agricultural Policy is quite a separate issue and unless otherwise stated this chapter refers only to industrial goods.) In addition industrial imports from the rest of Western Europe (EFTA) also come in duty-free. Dutiable goods (which mostly come from North America and from Asia) pay the same common external tariff wherever they enter the EC and the revenue goes to Brussels. Then duty-paid goods go into 'free circulation' inside the Community. This freedom of circulation can be suspended in some circumstances, which would be impossible if there was a truly single market with no barriers inside the EC.

The wish of member states to monitor tightly third-country imports coming in via EC neighbours is just one of the many reasons why a host of internal border controls and other barriers to trade still exist inside the Community. Indeed, as tariff policy was unavailable under EC and GATT rules, governments began to devise methods known as 'new protectionism' which were not specifically mentioned in the

GATT and the Treaty of Rome and so were 'grey' rather than blatantly illegal. Such measures included arbitrary rules for health and safety of products and subsidies to home producers, as well as 'Voluntary Export Restraints' (VERs). A VER means that a supplier (e.g. the Japanese car industry) 'agrees' to limit sales in your market as a result of your threats of even tougher exclusion. VERs could not be used to keep intra-EC imports out, but the spawning of separate measures at a national level had both indirect and direct effects to segment the EC market, and the ECs estimates of price dispersion inside the community show just how far it is from being a single market (see Cecchini (1988), Ch. 9).

3.3 THE COMMUNITY'S INSTRUMENTS FOR REMOVING NON-TARIFF BARRIERS

The Treaty of Rome commits member states to the concept of a common market and erects a joint decision-making process. Ultimate political responsibility in the EC broadly rests with the member states, i.e. the Council of Ministers. The Commission initiates proposals but (after consultation with the European Parliament) the Council of Ministers makes decisions, which go back to the Commission for implementation. The Treaty directly gives the Commission executive power in a limited field, notably on competition policy, controlling state aids, and abuses of position by public monopolies. The original provisions of the Treaty foreshadowed a true internal market but did not provide a way to implement it. When Jacques Delors took over as President of the EC Commission in 1984, the Community was in the doldrums. 'Eurosclerosis' was breeding 'Europessimism'. The proliferation of national trade policy measures risked undermining the established gains from economic integration and threatened to block all progress towards full economic union, a goal which the French and German governments had come to see as necessary for political reasons. After wide consultations Delors decided to launch the Internal Market programme as a vehicle to arrest the decline of the Community idea. The timing was admirable; a programme of deregulation suited both those who valued it for its own sake and those who saw it as a means to an end.

Accordingly, in 1985 the member states signed the Single European Act (effective from 1987) and the Commission published its White Paper on the Internal Market. The Single European Act

(SEA) contains a series of amendments to the Treaty of Rome; it binds signatories and is enforcible in the European Court of Justice in Luxembourg. A new article 8a in the Rome Treaty commits member states to create by 31 December 1992 an 'internal market' which 'shall comprise an area without frontiers in which the free movement of goods, persons, services and capital is ensured . . .' The amended Article 100a gives the Council of Ministers (i.e. the member states, not the Commission) power to harmonise national laws to achieve this end by a form of 'qualified majority voting' (54 out of a total of 76 votes are needed; states have voting power in proportion to size). The text of the SEA was accompanied by a 'Declaration on Article 8a' signed by a Conference of Representatives of Member States, which has two sentences. In the first the conference expresses 'its firm political will' to create the internal market before 1993 and specifically to implement the programme of the White Paper. But the second sentence declares that the 1992 deadline has no automatic legal effect, and a number of other 'declarations' state that governments must retain the right to take measures they see fit to combat terrorism, drugs and illegal movement of antiques.

The White Paper, unlike the SEA, is thus a political programme proposed by the Commission and then backed by the member states. But it creates no legal obligations until the directives it proposes are passed. Directives are 'laws' voted in the Council of Miniters – or in exceptional cases by the Commission – which then bind member states and determine what is permissible in national legislation. Member states must implement them or else the Court can declare national laws invalid. But the 1992 programme can only work if the EC Commission secures the cooperation of the member states, in supporting new policy initiatives and then in complying with what has been decided. If the member states were to baulk at the pace of change they could collectively sabotage the process they have themselves embarked on. The SEA by introducing 'qualified' majority voting on internal market issues explicitly removes the right of veto by individual member of states. It is, however, important to realise that in the past the Treaty of Rome has permitted majority voting on a number of issues, but this was not applied under the so-called 'Luxembourg Compromise' of 1966. That agreement was a purely informal one. The significance of the SEA is to symbolise a renewed political willingness to allow the provisions of the Treaty of Rome to be implemented in full. Acceptance of the White Paper reaffirms the

Commission's moral authority to ensure the creation of a true common market, a term not legally defined until Article 8a was spelled out.

The 1985 White Paper identifies the three major types of barriers as 'physical', 'technical' and 'fiscal', and it then specifies 300 new directives which were needed to secure its objective of removing frontiers (since consolidated to 279). It did not pinpoint the 300 most serious barriers to trade: it targeted the technical preconditions for the achievement of the specific aim of a Europe without frontiers. About 70 proposed directives concern animal and plant health: without harmonisation here one could not have generally open borders. Only a limited number of industrial harmonisation measures actually figure in the White Paper, but many more are logically entailed by the measures that are listed, and the system of majority voting can be invoked for any measure needed to realise the internal market.

Since 1985 the Commission has exploited several avenues to achieve the goal of an 'internal market without frontiers', in principle agreed by all member states. Article 100a makes harmonisation easier and the Commission has developed a new approach of minimising the amount of detail that needs to go into any Community directive. Only the most basic safety and performance requirements are legislated by the Community; any specification of the method of construction etc. is devolved to industry-based standards bodies such as the Comité Européen des Normes (CEN). The Commission has also sought to exploit the case law of the European Court of Justice to extend the principle of 'mutual recognition'.

The Commission has also gone directly to the Treaty of Rome in a number of instances – which worry member states – and used powers on competition which are vested directly in the Commission itself without being subject to approval by the Council of Ministers, e.g. on telecommunications (see below). Some member states worry that the Commission aims to develop a European industrial policy. This is unlikely without the support of member states. But the Commission is insisting on pursuing the full logic of the 1992 programme: if there is to be a single integrated internal market, there must be a vigorous competition policy, including merger policy, run by the Commission. European Court rulings support this and the member states have agreed to this principle. Merger proposals like GEC/Plessey are being 'pre-notified' to the Commission for scrutiny even before the establishment of formal rules for EC merger policy.

3.4   THE ECONOMIC MOTIVES FOR THE 1992 PROGRAMME: FEARS OF FRAGMENTATION AND 'EUROSCLEROSIS'

The aims of the 1992 programme are twofold: first to eliminate the direct cost of border delays and red tape, etc., and secondly as a result of this to transform the competitive mentality of European business. We can distinguish the following levels of costs caused by NTBs:

(a) The direct cost of unnecessary regulation, border delays, etc., is a dead-weight cost to everyone.
(b) By affecting the volume of trade NTBs might be depriving European firms of opportunities to exploit economies of scale, as well as consumers of freedom of choice.
(c) Most controversially, NTBs which impose small direct costs might foster a cartellistic oligopoly environment in which the dynamic benefits of competition are lost.

Even a very small percentage excess cost due to unnecessary regulation adds up to a large absolute amount. Red tape may tie up domestic production as well as goods crossing borders, and unlike tariffs there is not even any revenue raised. The British government largely sees the single market in terms of a general process of deregulation which affects business generally, not just the cost of crossing borders. The burden is further magnified by indirect effects if it leads firms to have too many small plants and too short production runs. But are Eurosize mega-plants really so much more efficient? If so why don't firms set them up anyway? Geroski doubts there are huge economies of scale to be had from consolidation of firms and plants. Lundgren (1969) first observed that if you could cut costs by more than, say, 10 per cent by producing for the European market, you would do so in the presence of any trade barriers lower than that value, so the economies of scale argument requires an explanation of how small barriers could stop big gains.

However, the achievement of economies of scale requires an aggressive attitude to cross-border competition that many European firms simply do not have, either because they are simply undynamic or else because they fear that entering someone else's 'home market' would provoke retaliation whether by the rival firm or by government – in the form of protective subsidies or other NTBs. By opening markets and restricting governments' ability to bail out lame-duck firms, the 1992 programme hopes to change this market-driven segmentation. EC Commission economists consider that it is this third effect that gives us the bulk of the 5–6 per cent of GDP gains that are hoped for.

These gains will only be achieved at the expense of considerable transition costs, but it has always been the position of mainstream economics that such costs are a necessary price for economic evolution. There is also another problem in getting all the gains from eliminating NTBs: not all NTBs are simply trade barriers. We want to do away with unnecessary regulations but we may have difficulty in eliminating barriers that cause artificial segmentation without throwing some healthy babies out with the bathwater. It is much easier to categorise NTBs than to identify them and assess their effects in practice. Baldwin (1970) in the classic work on NTBs notes that all kinds of domestic policy interventions, including taxes, tax exemptions and subsidies, can be 'non-tariff distortions' and indirectly affect trade. Any government intervention in the economy can affect trade as well as having a real or apparent legitimate purpose. But some non-tariff measures, such as tight product specifications, bring some benefits to consumers. As Geroski points out, national standards often respond to a distinct national market need. Indeed Article 36 of the Rome Treaty even allows trade barriers for such purposes as the 'protection of health and life . . .' but only so long as they are not 'disguised restrictions on trade'. European consumer lobbies broadly support free trade because of the lower prices and wider choice it brings; they argue that it is usually possible to distinguish phoney and genuine consumer protection rules.

Baldwin suggests while trade liberalisation must not concern itself only with measures directly affecting trade, it should only aim to bother about measures which 'significantly' distort (whether to promote or restrict) trade. We do not start from a 'perfect' *laissez-faire* free-trade world to which we might aspire to return. Any internal market programme could not have been operationalised without choosing priorities. No one imagines the EC should harmonise everything, let alone impose 'optimal' policies on all members. But it can guarantee the maintainance of predictable and stable policies so that member states cannot arbitrarily change the rules on their neighbours: the removal of frontiers is intended to symbolise the guarantee.

It can be argued that the greatest post-war achievements of the EC and of GATT have not been so much their ability to reduce tariffs as the assurance given that tariffs would never be increased again. Would-be exporters could safely plan their investments and exploit economies of scale for sales to the entire world market, so long as their competitive edge exceeded existing tariff barriers. If they did well in foreign markets they did not have to fear sudden increases in tariffs. Within the EC the Treaty of Rome by actually abolishing tariffs gave a tighter guarantee of tariff-free access to neighbouring markets. In this vital aspect, the rules of the trading game were rigidly fixed. Owen's work (1983) argues the importance of economies of scale in realising gains from the creation of the EC. But his numerical examples show that most of the economies of scale he postulates could still have been profitably exploited even with the tariffs in place. Can we justify the importance of tariff reductions? Yes, if exporters experience a boost in 'animal spirits' with the certain knowledge that no retaliation would be forthcoming if they succeeded in export markets. Firms with a will to exploit this, above all in Germany, did so. But the rise of intra-EC NTBs, above all the rising fear of them, creates a wholly new situation. The threat of imposing new NTBs is crucial. Externally, the Japanese agree 'voluntarily' to restrict sales of cars or VCRs because they know that European governments will not allow their domestic industries to collapse. There has been an implicit understanding that the UK government will not let Rover disappear, nor the French Renault, nor the Italians Fiat; and other EC firms understand the implied rules of competition. Any outsider must respect certain understandings about the minimum market share of the national champion in certain key industries. These understandings are implicit and uncertain. Firms are always ready to go to their governments for assistance against 'unfair' competition. A new entrant to a market will generally find it prudent to respect the prices and core market share of the incumbent. One of the most remarkable examples of a business being open about its attitudes is Philips who told *The Financial Times* (25 July 1988) that their 'rightful' European market share in consumer electronics products was 20–25 per cent. Other European producers are mindful of these set positions.

The Commission is anxious to introduce much stricter monitoring and control of subsidy measures, above all to prevent them being introduced at the discretion of governments whenever a local firm is in difficulties. For example, £100m worth of subsidies pre-announced and pre-committed to a given programme may be less significant than an Industry Ministry's ability to summon quickly a few tens of millions whenever a firm it wants to back is in trouble, so measuring the amount of subsidies is not all that needs to be monitored. The internal market case says that the firms must be sure that if they can get ahead of the pack by innovation or cost-cutting they will be guaranteed to scoop the benefits of this across Europe, but if they lag behind they will not be bailed out.

In mainstream economics, subsidies are seen as hurting the country introducing them (except in hard-to-identify 'strategic' products – see Krugman (1987)); but here we see that subsidies in one country can distort investment in other countries by creating a fear of market exclusion. (Beyond the 1992 debate we can surely argue that this threat is a highly damaging effect of placing quotas or anti-dumping duties on external imports from NICs wherever they have seemed to succeed, e.g. Korean VCRs.)

In sum, the justification for the internal market programme was a genuine fear that protectionism in external trade threatened to spread within the EC itself. We now turn to the application of the 1992 programme to a number of specific issues.

3.5 TACKLING NON-TARIFF BARRIERS IN PRACTICE

In this section we examine in more detail some of the main substantive problems to be resolved by 1993, with the exception of fiscal barriers which are being dealt with elsewhere. In view of the importance of competition to the 1992 process, private barriers to trade are separately highlighted, though one feature of the argument is that very often legal rules provide a cover for anti-competitive behaviour by firms.

3.5.1 Administrative costs and border controls

The abolition of all physical frontier barriers is the basic aim of the White Paper and Article 8a of the revised Rome Treaty. The wording covers people as well as goods, and the White Paper explicitly recognises that this implies the tightening of external border controls and more effective national police controls and cooperation, e.g. on terrorism, though in their 'declarations' the member governments gave themselves escape clauses.

The idea of reducing red tape is an appealing one, and its importance was for many years over-stressed through the currency given to a quasi-mythical estimate that unnecessary paperwork for intra-EC

trade and border delays cost 5–10 per cent of the value of intra-EC
trade. The Cecchini study suggests that trade-related red tape costs
about 2 per cent of the value of intra-EC trade on average according
to consultants, or 0.2–0.3 per cent of Community GDP. Border
delays can prolong journey times extraordinarily; a 750-mile truck
trip from London within the UK took 36 hours, but 750 miles to
Milan took 58 hours – plus the Channel crossing. For small firms the
unpredictability of delays as well as the absolute cost can be significant. The sources of administrative burdens on trade are manifold,
including the need to ensure correct tax treatment, the collection of
statistics, regulations governing transport, the existence of national
measures affecting imports from third countries coming via EC
members, and the monitoring of a variety of technical or health
regulations at borders.

But the basic finding of the Cecchini study is that prices of identical
or equivalent goods – net of tax – differ from market to market by
much more than can be explained by these transactions costs. Standard deviations of prices across the community are typically 15–20
per cent of average prices. Something else is segmenting markets,
something which is facilitated, however, by the existence of clearly
demarcated borders.

Widely different national tax regimes clearly require border controls to stop tax avoidance. And some form of fiscal approximation is
implied by eliminating frontiers. This is being dealt with elsewhere in
this book so here we will be very brief. Despite much debate, VAT
harmonisation is a much less difficult matter than dealing with excise
duties on alcohol and tobacco. There are a number of possible
solutions. The big problems lie in designing the best bureaucratic
procedures to ensure that commercial movements of taxable goods
can be monitored via normal tax returns and not at borders. The
British government in its dispute (see FT 9 September 1988) with the
Commission makes a lot of sense in arguing that the Cockfield
proposals propose more harmonisation of VAT than is really needed,
but at the same time the UK fails to recognise that for the rest of the
Community elimination of VAT checks at borders, not just their
simplification, has deep symbolic importance. In any case, for individuals, 'duty-free', i.e. tax-free, allowances should be abolished
after 1992, but citizens would have unlimited rights to shop across
borders paying only the tax in the country of purchase. This will be a
major additional force integrating markets.

Transport regulations can potentially affect trade in goods quite severely, since countries, e.g. Germany, with highly regulated national systems also require foreign lorries to apply for a restricted number of permits before allowing them to carry goods, under a system of reciprocal bilateral agreements, which the Community has long tolerated. The UK and the Netherlands on the other hand admit unlimited numbers of each other's lorries. The Germans have now agreed to a community-wide liberalisation of access, providing there is a general tightening of safety standards etc. in road transport. Striking as the transport barriers are, however, there is little evidence that they have a disproportionate impact on intra-EC trade as opposed to raising costs within the regulated markets. The introduction of the new 'Single Administrative Document' has now eased the movement of goods, and certain bizzare controls on transport (such as taxing fuel in lorry tanks) should be eliminated by 1993.

Border checks also affect 'third-country' goods. The Treaty of Rome (Article 9) allows any external imported good to circulate freely once it has paid the common external tariff, just as if it were an EC-made good; but Article 115 of the Treaty allows the Commission to authorise in some circumstances individual member states that retain separate national quantitative restrictions on external imports to demand licenses for the import of third-country goods entering via an intra-EC border. For example France has long had its own import quotas on colour TVs from Japan (legally recognised by Brussels) and the Commission has authorised it to ban Japanese TVs from another EC country entering, e.g. via the UK, without a permit issued in Paris. Until the Community can get a single unified system of external NTBs, there will still be a need for internal barriers to stop what is known as 'trade deflection'. Commission officials argue privately that there *must* be a totally unified external trade regime by 1993. The White Paper (para. 35) recognises this but it has been little discussed by governments. But there can be no true internal market until it also applies to the output of plants of foreign investors: the French have recently disputed the right of free circulation to Nissan cars made or assembled in the UK. By strategically placing their investments all over Europe, the Japanese are clearly hoping that governments will see a common interest in allowing free circulation for their own 'home-made Japanese' products, as Article 9 lays down they should. But there is a real risk that a 'solution' will take the form of Japanese and other firms tacitly agreeing through trade associations to swap information and carve up markets as if national licensing controls were still in place.

Technical and health regulations are our next major theme, but at this point we should note that for many continental countries, especially France, it is customary to monitor such rules at the border, rather than say at the point of sale or use as is common in the UK. In France you cannot import a car unless you satisfy inspectors that it conforms to French norms; in the UK monitoring is when the car is registered for use, hence the relative ease with which France can actually or seemingly use border controls to stop goods entering the country.

3.5.2   Technical barriers

Cecchini (1988) estimates that although only 0.2 to 0.3 per cent of EC GDP is wasted on border measures, the cost of 'measures affecting all production' is a full 2.0 to 2.4 per cent. Of these measures, the most obvious are standards and technical regulations designed not to improve products, but to keep foreign suppliers out. Much confusion exists in this area. Three concepts exist. Standards are merely sets of agreed blueprints which people may voluntarily adopt or not. They are drawn up by non-governmental bodies, such as the British Standards Institution, the Deutsche Industrie-Norm (DIN), the European Standards Committee (CEN) or the International Standards Organisation (ISO). Technical regulations are laws, which lay down required design or performance characteristics, sometimes but not always based on existing standards. 'Testing and certification' procedures are quite distinct from the norms themselves. In the limit, you may enforce the same standards as your neighbours, but insist that every imported item be tested to destruction! Despite anecdotal evidence, standards rarely pose problems but regulations and certification procedures commonly do. However, discussions with industry and government representatives suggest that the bulk of trade is unaffected by barriers. British standards are rarely compulsory, and experts claim that they are more flexibly defined than some continental equivalents. In France the overwhelming majority of official standards are identical to ISO norms, and only about 3 per cent are compulsory (other than for public purchasing contracts). In special cases they are used as trade barriers, e.g. to halt the inflow of Italian refrigerators in the early 1980s. Industrial standards are very important in Germany. Here the law imposes very vague technical and safety requirements, but asserts that anything certified as conforming to DIN standards must be deemed acceptable. Access to the German market is further impeded by the unwillingness of private business, including insurers, to accept anything without a DIN certificate issued by the (private) German testing agencies.

There is considerable evidence that the costs of complying with a variety of different clearly known and unambiguous standards is only modestly problematic to large manufacturers. (See, for example, appendices to House of Lords (1982).) One has only to look carefully at the windows of a typical imported Japanese car to see the etched symbols indicating how many different regulatory regimes the glass simultaneously satisfies. In fact for most specifications, the European car industry and the Commission have agreed common regulations: what has not been agreed is the system for giving vehicles certificates confirming they comply. A standard model must be tested to destruction; then the manufacturer can issue 'Type Approval Certificates' to each individual vehicle declaring it has been made in the same way as the tested sample. Procedures for issuing the certificates differ. France insists that Japanese cars be first tested and then each individual vehicle monitored for certification at the port of entry. The inspectors (at the docks) are unofficially instructed to check the paperwork at a pace that will give the Japanese 3 per cent of the French market. Other arrangements monitor the 11 per cent share of the UK market that Japanese producers 'voluntarily' accept. Technical standards are just an element in a more subtle system. The number of different sub-models of car sold in Europe is due as much to marketing considerations as to trade barriers. It is very rare for standards to be imposed on firms by governments. One interesting example relates to colour TVs. The French have long had the idiosyncratic SECAM system for CTV, unlike the rest of Europe's PAL system. In part this was promoted by the French government but since its inception, new twists on insulating the French market, e.g. the requirement to have a 'peritelevision' socket, have come from the industry itself. But the 'French' TV industry consists of Thomson, a French firm, and Philips's French subsidiary who have been just as active in creating a distinctive high-price market. New technology makes it easy for firms to develop multi-standard chips in TV sets and the French market is now vulnerable to Sony sets made in the UK. But Sony has little interest in destabilising the French market; a small slice of a high-margin market is better than a costly battle for market share. We too often treat technical barriers as if they exist to protect 'national champions' against outsiders, whereas in fact the national champions are often multinationals doing all they can to consolidate product differentiation and market segmentation to reduce the cost of oligopolistic rivalry.

The Community is pressing ahead with its new approach to harmonisation. As we noted above this involves using majority voting under Article 100a and relying increasingly on the Commission's own power both to apply powers vested in it by the Treaty and to get the European Court to build on recent case law, notably the 1978 Cassis de Dijon case. Here the court struck down a German ruling excluding this beverage for not having enough alcohol in it to satisfy the German definition of a liqueur! The Court ruled that in general whatever was legally allowed in one member state should be acceptable in any other, and the onus was on any excluding country to prove a genuine public health type case otherwise. This doctrine of 'mutual recognition', rather than impose uniformity, has become the Community's touchstone. It is trickiest in the area of testing and certification where some may fear that though quality standards in some countries look good on paper, testing procedures are lax. There is therefore some need for harmonisation to be imposed from Brussels, but under the new approach the Commission and Council will only seek to determine essential safety criteria and devolve further specifications to standards bodies such as the Comité Européen des Normes (CEN).

The problem one always faces in these situations is as follows: if harmonised standards are economically profitable why doesn't industry adopt them anyway? Common standards are 'public goods' which benefit firms who support the costs and those who do not alike, and so the market will not provide enough of it. But it is also true, as Geroski points out in this volume, that there are strong interests against harmonisation. Sometimes this is from the anti-competitive instincts of firms noted above. In other cases national differentiation serves a real purpose. For example, in the well-documented example of the food industry (see Cecchini (1988)), big gains mainly come from cost reductions if rules are dropped which require only certain ingredients to be used; it is less easy to measure the offsetting loss of value to consumers.

The Cecchini study found it impossible to estimate the total cost of non-harmonised standards to industry. They are obviously very important in certain cases, but usually only when they interact with another factor. The most important of these we have not touched on so far is public procurement.

Table 3.1   Competition in public contracting

	France	Germany	UK
Estimated % import penetration[1]	16	12	4
% of open tenders[2]	4	5	6
% of contracts awarded on cost only[3]	9	1	5
% of contracts advertised in *OJEC*[4]	16	22	29

Notes:
1. Estimates by purchasers of the breakdown of origin of goods ordered by value.
2. Percentage of 4,000 contracts studied where any bidder could apply (as opposed to contract by private negotiation or via restricted list of approved bidders).
3. Percentage by value of contracts where bid selected by price alone.
4. Percentage by value of contracts advertised in Official Journal of the European Community.

NB: 80% of contracts studied were large enough for advertising in *OJEC* to be compulsory.

Source: Atkins (1988), various tables.

3.5.3   Public procurement and hidden subsidies

In this area, we can be quite confident that the Commission is not 'crying wolf'. The Treaty of Rome in principle applies equally to goods bought by government bodies (apart from defence), but the Community legislation designed to give it effect has been feeble and fitfully applied. Directives have long existed requiring public authorities to advertise their purchases in the *Official Journal of the European Community*, but evidence shows that barely a quarter of such contracts are so advertised, and the proportion of public sector purchases going to suppliers outside the home country is astonishingly low (aside from Belgium), although the available data may be underestimates of the indirect import content of what is apparently bought from a 'domestic' supplier (who may well not be the producer). Directives exempted water supply, power and telecommunication, but the Commission and the Council have agreed to end the exclusions with action promised by mid-1990. There is a long way to go, however, before a truly unified market can exist.

The data in Table 3.1 from a survey of 4,000 public sector contracts by W.S. Atkins for the Cecchini Report indicate the lack of international and even domestic competition in public procurement contracting. One equally remarkable statistic is the fact that a third of all contracts on which Atkins obtained information had only one bidder.

Britain, France and Germany seem equally restrictive. Apparent import penetration is very low. Bidding is generally restricted only to a small number of approved suppliers and in general the bigger the contract the fewer the bidders. Contracts that should be advertised across the EC are not. There is very little incentive for price competition.

The reasons for this segmentation are complex. Political motives lead public authorities to instruct agencies not to buy abroad, and in addition there are powerful economic and institutional factors which in any case would militate against a high direct import content. Some political factors are evident: there are conspicuous goods (e.g. the crockery in the House of Commons or ministerial cars), there are 'strategic' goods, and there are products produced in politically sensitive regions. Local authorities sometimes want to favour goods produced regionally.

We must distinguish between the purchase of standardised readily tradeable goods (e.g. cars or basic office supplies), and purchases of custom-made specialised equipment. For the former case, there is some evidence that public authorities could have saved money by going directly to foreign suppliers instead of buying at home, but Atkins' data suggests that the public sector was not systematically paying any more than the going rate in the domestic market; public sector prices simply reflected the segmentation of private markets. The reason for this seems to be that the supply of simple goods to the public sector is 'contestable', with easy entry for potential competitors even when few firms are actually in the market. Market competition (or is it collusion?) inside the domestic market ensures equivalence of prices between public and private sector purchases of nationally produced goods, and between home and foreign goods within the national market, even where cross-border differentials exist. The public authorities by approaching foreign wholesalers could in principle make savings for themselves and contribute to greater inter-country competition. But for run-of-the-mill goods, there is little evidence that the public sector adds to fragmentation of markets except where the considerations referred to above come into play. The key point is that evidence is sparse on potential cost savings from searching abroad. Even with a database of several thousand contracts the consultants had difficulty ascertaining true 'prices'.

Most orders are mixed bundles of goods and services differing in quality, quantity and terms of supply (who carries stocks of spares etc.). There is reason to believe that public sector buyers conservatively prefer long-standing relations with established 'reliable' local suppliers, but there is surprisingly little evidence that they shop around any less than large private sector buyers who would also decline to switch their business every time a 'cowboy' supplier comes along. There are thus quasi-commercial reasons to explain why in most countries public authorities reported that open tendering was a rare method of purchase, and that price alone was not the selection criterion.

For really big contracts, preparing and evaluating bids is expensive and we can expect few suppliers. In the Atkins data, the category of contracts where there was only one bidder had the highest average value. For technologically complex one-off purchases of expensive equipment, goods, medical technology, telephone exchanges, power generation equipment, defence and perhaps some construction materials, there are a handful of accredited suppliers who are authorised to tender and with whom specifications and terms are subject to bargaining rather than market forces. This is largely inevitable where economies of scale are substantial in both the development of new products and in production. It would be impossibly costly to have a dozen makers of telephone exchanges in every country. But industrial buyers are aware of the advantages of having even a second source of supplies, provided that is there is an element of genuine competition. With public procurement there has often been a 'club' mentality in which the public agency identifies its own interests with that of the health of the national suppliers, and neighbours keep out. Lack of competition can be very costly, and there are a number of important European industries where the only way simultaneously to obtain the full benefits of economies of scale and have enough firms to act as competitors and potential competitors is to go to a European-wide market; power generation equipment, railway locomotives and telecommunications are examples. The telecommunications industry is becoming Europeanised. The big danger is that having abandoned the unviable idea of national champions supported by public procurement, we may move towards a cartel of European champions. Of course the way out is to allow moderately free access to non-EC firms; but there are very severe transitional risks. In the case of telecommunications equipment, EC prices vary from two to five times an estimated 'competitive' world market price (see

Cecchini (1988)). Here we see the core of the 1992 dilemma. There are huge gains to be had if subjecting the public procurement industries to competition can get their prices down by even a fraction of this margin, but there is a very severe crisis in store for those parts of the industry least capable of competing.

The consultants calculated the maximum possible benefits of opening up public procurement given existing cost conditions. They identified a 'static' gain from increasing the level of public sector imports to the same share as in the rest of the economy with ensuing price savings, a competition effect from the need for domestic suppliers in consequence to cut prices (and by implication short-run costs) to match imports, and a restructuring effect as plants were closed and economies of scale realised. The latter effect (the least quantifiable) came to about half the total estimate of 0.5 per cent of EC GDP. To this one could add, optimistically, the true dynamic effects of faster innovation if that is triggered off by more competition.

The logic of the whole process is that where firms find themselves subject to intensified competition, the government should not protect them by subsidies. Indeed protective public procurement is just one method of state support for particular industries. Article 92 of the Rome Treaty bans state aids which 'distort competition' and 'affect trade'. Some exceptions are permitted and the Commission has started to demand more information from member states to ensure such aids conform with the rules. Article 90 of the Rome Treaty allows the Commission without the Council of Ministers to issue directives preventing public enterprises from obstructing trade, and this power has been used for telecommunications terminal equipment. There has been a challenge in the European Court from several states to the Commission's use of its direct powers in this way on terminal equipment, but the Commission is expected to win, and a legal victory would enhance the political legitimacy of such powers.

Pelkmans and Winters (1988) fear that rampant national subsidies could simply replace barriers on public procurement etc. that have been removed. A further fear is that cartels of 'European champions' will not only be able to avoid competition but will demand big subsidies from the Community, especially since more open public procurement inside the EC will inevitably allow easier entry for non-EC firms. The proposals on public procurement permit but do not prevent a certain measure of 'community preference' *vis-a-vis* the outside world. Some in the Community fear this will not be enough protection; others, especially in the USA, fear there will be too much.

The benefits of a cold-shower effect would be dramatic if it succeeded, but the downside risk is of course that when prices fell some firms just could not adapt. Economists are inclined to say that resources should therefore just move out of those sectors. Most European politicians, and especially the Commission, cannot ignore the social consequences, but the essential message coming from EC President Delors is that the right way to deal with the social side-effects of the 1992 programme is through an intensified social policy, not through industrial policy. This call for a 'social Europe' is being taken up by the Germans and the French, both of whom share a somewhat un-Thatcherite vision of a social market economy in Europe after 1992.

3.6 THE ROLE OF PRIVATE FIRMS

The theme we have been developing so far is that it is wrong to see NTBs inside the EC as walls erected by protectionist governments against which tough macho firms beat in vain in their fierce efforts to enter new markets. Far from it: state NTBs are often just part of the structure which firms impose on markets to keep competition manageable. This is in addition to the natural barriers of taste and language differences that lead firms to produce different models for each national market, most obviously for cars but visible also for, say, washing machines (e.g. top-loaders only in France).

Textbooks too often teach us that oligopolistic industries are inherently prone to cut-throat competition. Modern theories and empirical observation suggest the opposite (see Schmalensee (1988), also Holmes (1978)). You don't start price wars unless you can be sure to win, and everyone is happy to have mechanisms in place which restrain price competition. Elementary economics shows that if firms can succeed in segmenting markets where local demand conditions (i.e. price elasticities) differ, more profit can be made through price discrimination than by charging a uniform price across Europe. A fascinating question in this area is always as follows: why do so few economic actors try to exploit or challenge such arrangements either by cross-border arbitrage or by going to court when this is blocked?

The case of consumer electronics (CE) in France is interesting. The inflow of some Korean and Japanese products (but not all) is regulated by EC Article 115 decisions, but prices of all CE products, European or Asian, tend to be high in France. The reason seems to be that the system in place permits extra profit to be garnered from consumers, and that part of it is distributed to other economic agents who might have an interest in breaking up the price ring. Retailers can be encouraged not to buy direct more cheaply. The French discount chain FNAC has actually taken the government to court to challenge price controls on books – but have stated (in an interview with the author) that they would not try to buy TVs and hi-fi cheap in the UK for re-sale in France, where under the present system their margins are high. Everyone is locked in. The local French producers (Thomson and Philips) are given licences to import a quota of cheap goods from Asia; the Japanese are allowed guaranteed market access for a certain quantity at high prices; and vertical integration for after-sales service etc. mitigates the conflict of interest with retailers. A potential entrant (i.e. someone selling a small amount contemplating enlargement of sales by price cuts, e.g. Amstrad) would have to achieve a very large increase in market share to compensate for a per unit cut in profit margins. One large multinational TV manufacturer refused to supply an international retail chain with TVs from the UK at UK prices for sale in France because it would cut their profit margins by 50 per cent.

The distribution system plays a crucial part in market segmentation. Arbitrage to even out prices is made very difficult if firms insist on customers going only through 'authorised' dealers. Respect for distribution channels even affects items like bulk chemicals where product differentiation is impossible.

The interest of business lies in removing those barriers to trade that increase costs but not in stimulating all-out price competition in European markets. As we have seen in the discussion of technical barriers, the current philosophy of harmonisation is inextricably linked with liberalisation and deregulation. Mutual recognition implies a certain 'competition among rules' (see Padoa-Schioppa (1987)) so firms have a certain freedom to opt for whichever standards regime in Europe suits them best, causing inevitable pressures for governments to level the degree of control downwards to the minimum levels that will have been commonly agreed. Even though many NTBs are themselves reactions to business pressure it is clear that a general wave of deregulation is likely to be in business interest. We therefore find considerable enthusiasm for the concept of the open market but systematic reservations by business where their own, sometimes transnational, interests are at stake. Hence, as Cecchini (1988) argues, full implementation requires an invigorated European-wide competition policy to enforce competition and inhibit cross-border mergers whose aim is to forestall transnational competition. The European Court has affirmed that mergers are implicitly covered by the Rome Treaty's assignment of competition policy to the EC Commission; member governments have to agree only on the details of implementation, though unanimity is required. Some disputes remain, e.g. about the threshold for reference to Brussels, and also about the extent to which the Commission may trade off industrial policy goals 'promoting technical or economic progress' (Article 85) against the need for more competition.

3.7 THE OVERALL PICTURE

The Cecchini study supported very strongly the view that the direct costs imposed on business of NTBs were quantitatively small, but that major effects (5–6 per cent of EC GDP) could follow if the behavioural response of firms to the small shifts in certain cost parameters is substantial. If these competitive factors alter, some extra economies of scale could well be realised, but the gain will not necessarily be retained as higher profits. Of the 5–6 per cent gain in GDP much is likely to go to consumers if competition intensifies. The logic of the argument is that firms are only likely to be able to capture the benefits to the extent that they cut their costs more than the average, unless of course the 1992 exercise manages to stimulate faster growth all round. Business psychology is not just a matter of calculating the costs of NTBs to the last ECU. Firms apparently do perceive that removal of NTBs will create a new market dynamism, perhaps allowing the development of hitherto unsuspected markets and product niches. In Keynesian terms the 1992 project is trying to boost the animal spirits of entrepreneurs, hoping that the removal of a series of regulatory barriers will have a disproportionate effect on their strategies.

A survey of business opinion, commissioned as part of the Cecchini exercise (see Nerb (1988)), showed an interesting pattern of expectations about the consequences of removing NTBs, which some observers would consider over-optimistic, but which nevertheless is logically consistent and would, if acted upon, lead to a stimulation of activity. Firms across Europe consistently reported that removal of all NTBs would reduce their total costs directly by about 2 per cent. On average they expected sales volume to rise by 5 per cent. This number varied only slightly across countries and sectors, suggesting that in most cases intra-industry adjustment was likely rather than whole sectors going out of business. Firms generally expected to lose market share at home but to gain by more intra-EC exports. This implies an expectation of a boost to overall aggregate demand. Now a pure monetarist or supply-sider could argue that the rise in productivity caused by lower costs would automatically generate additional aggregate demand. The boost could come from a higher real money supply due to lower prices or from higher profitability. A Keynesian would naturally be sceptical of the former effect, and any economist will have doubts about the consequences for medium-term profitability of enhanced internal competition. The Cecchini report (1988, p. 3) is being disingenuous in observing that the cost of NTBs amounts to 25 per cent of average profit margins if most of the savings are to be passed on in lower prices. Hence, one can see the reason why EC Commission economists argue so strongly that in order to sustain the demand expectations effect on the part of firms, some of the anti-inflationary bonus from price reductions should be 'spent' by governments in the form of some reflation. This suggestion will remain controversial, as is J. Delors's idea that the community must create a 'social Europe'. He has in mind an internal social market economy where workers' rights are enhanced and there is no temptation to compete internally by levelling down employment conditions.

It seems certain that the psychological component in the exercise is crucial. The removal of frontier controls is symbolic but arguably essential. Firms must be able to believe that governments are sincere in their commitment not to reinstate national NTBs whenever it might be expedient to do so. One can therefore sympathise with the Commission's view that once the Cockfield programme has been accepted, the rejection of even part of the package would undermine its credibility.

What are the chances of the 1992 deadline being met? By November 1988 the Commission expected to have produced 90 per cent of a now reduced target of 279 directives. About 30 per cent of the 279 were actually in law, and another 10 per cent were agreed by the Council and Commission, subject only to approval by the European Parliament. Naturally most progress has been made in the basic and easier areas of technical standards, with framework directives on pressure vessels, toys, construction materials, and electromagnetic compatibility, and faster progress on food law than some experts expected. Service sectors have also seen significant development, especially transport, but also financial services. As we noted, agreement in principle exists on public procurement. The Commission's strategy is naturally to get agreement on the less sensitive items first, to build up pressure on the others, the percentage figures for implementation deliberately exaggerating how near the final goal is. The one area where virtually no progress at all has been made is on free movement of persons. The Commission insists, however, that a binding commitment exists to create a 'Europe without Frontiers'. They argue that:

> The Cecchini Report makes it clear that to achieve the full economic benefits of the completed Internal Market frontier controls must be removed completely: any pretext for retaining a frontier control for a specific purpose, even if arguments could be advanced to support it if looked at in isolation, will preserve or create the machinery for interrupting the free flow of goods, services, capital and people which the Single Act commits us to achieving.
>
> (EC, 1988a, p. 12)

Perhaps other governments will use Mrs Thatcher's obstinacy as an excuse to renege on their political promises (and treaty commitment) to create an area without frontiers by 1993, but the Commission is gambling on public and business opinion forcing the pace. The aim of a Europe without frontiers is a Pandora's box of immense proportions. Technically it requires minimal loss of economic or political sovereignty, beyond what was originally in the Treaty of Rome, merely the exercise of that sovereignty by government agencies away from borders in such a way that the Treaty obligations can be rigorously enforced by the courts. For the internal market to work requires intense inter-governmental collaboration on economic policy. Supporters of European Union see the creation of an unstoppable political agenda: the single market once in place will create problems that can only be solved by community-wide policies, and Jacques Delors is already expanding the agenda. European public opinion may well begin to ask why there is not a European currency and a European government if there is a European economy. Clearly Mrs Thatcher is afraid of this; Britain can veto any further developments that require unanimous consent, e.g. on monetary unification, but only at the potential political cost of losing some of the liberalisation she seeks. Economists will differ on the extent to which having a single market makes currency union vital, but the important point to remember is that the 1992 programme is not simply a technical exercise in deregulation, reducing administrative costs. It is a grand gamble designed to alter the competitive mentality of European firms in a way which the Treaty of Rome itself only partly achieved, and it is also intended to concentrate the European political mind. Most commentators, especially in the UK, remain sceptical, but if the operation succeeds the consequences will be far more dramatic than the ability of a few yuppies to use the same car-phone in Blackpool and Brindisi.

References

Atkins, W.S. (1988) 'The "cost of non-Europe" in public procurement, *Research on the 'Cost of Non-Europe', Basic Findings Volume 5 Part A*, EC Commission, Brussels.
Baldwin, R.E. (1970) *Non-tariff Distortions of International Trade*, Brookings, Washington.
Cecchini, P. (1988) *The European Challenge: 1992*, Gower, London.
Commission of the European Communities, (March 1988) 'The Economics of 1992', *European Economy*, special edition, 35, pp. 1–222.
Holmes, P. (1978) *Industrial Pricing and Devaluation*, Macmillan, London.
House of Lords, Select Committee on the European Communities, *17th Report of 1981–2: The Internal Market*, HMSO.
Krugman, P. (ed.) (1987) *Strategic Trade Policy and the New International Economics*, MIT Press, Cambridge, Mass.
Lundgren, N. (1969) 'Customs unions of industrialised Western European countries', in G. Denton (ed.), *Economic Integration in Europe*, Weidenfeld & Nicholson, London.
Nerb, G. (1988) 'The completion of the internal market: a survey of European industry's perceptions of the likely effects', *Research on the 'Cost of Non-Europe', Basic Findings Volume 3*, EC Commission, Brussels.
Owen, N. (1983) *Economies of Scale, Competitiveness and Trade Patterns within the European Community*, Clarendon Press, Oxford.
Padoa-Schioppa, T. (1987) *Efficiency, Stability, and Equity*, European Commission, Brussels.
Pelkmans, J. and Winters, A. (1988) *Europe's Domestic Market*, Routledge & Kegan Paul, London.
Schmalensee, R. (September 1988) 'Industrial economics, an overview', *Economic Journal*, Vol. 98, No. 392, pp. 643–81.

4 International Trade and the Internal Market

Anthony J. Venables

Removal of barriers to trade is at the heart of the European Community's completion of the internal market programme. Tariffs and quotas on intra-Community trade have almost entirely been dismantled, but other non-tariff barriers remain. Some of these increase the costs of undertaking intra-Community trade, while others amount to actual or virtual prohibitions of certain trades.

This chapter outlines some approaches to analysing the possible effects of removal of these barriers. Any economic analysis of the removal of trade barriers must proceed in two stages. First, it must establish what the barriers are, and why they matter. How big are they, who do they effect, and what are the *direct* effects of their removal? Second, having identified and, if possible, quantified the barriers, analysis may turn to their *indirect* effects, that is the induced changes in trade, production, consumption and economic welfare brought about by their removal.

Section 4.1 is devoted to identifying the direct effects of trade barriers. Existing barriers are itemised, and the proposals for their removal are discussed. It is convenient to divide the direct effects of trade barriers into three categories. First, barriers impose private costs on exporters and importers and hence reduce the incentive to trade. A measure of this private cost is the 'tariff equivalent' of the barrier, which expresses the cost of the barrier as a percentage of the value of trade. For example, the effect on an exporter of having to spend 1 ECU on customs paperwork for every 100 ECU of exports is equivalent to the firm facing a 1 per cent tariff on its exports; an absolute prohibition on trade is equivalent to the firm facing an infinite tariff.

Second, barriers may directly incur social costs, so direct benefits follow from their removal. We shall call these the resource costs of the barrier. Thus a 1 per cent import tariff has zero resource cost because the private cost of the tariff on firms is offset by the benefit of tariff revenue accruing to the government. However, paperwork

51

amounting to a 1 per cent tariff equivalent also has a resource cost of 1 per cent of the value of trade.

Measurement of the first two of these direct effects is possible, if somewhat speculative. The third direct effect of trade barriers is far more difficult to quantify. This effect is the fact that trade barriers tend to segment national markets, and thereby permit firms to price discriminate between different countries, exploiting monopoly power in markets where they are relatively dominant. It seems clear that the European market for many products – for example motor cars – is strongly segmented, with wide price differentials observed between countries. However, it is difficult to assess the extent to which a particular trade barrier contributes to market segmentation or to know whether a particular package of policy measures will destroy segmentation and create a single 'unified' market.

Once the direct effects of removal of barriers have been identified, analysis can turn to the indirect effects. In order to analyse these an economic model is required. The economist's traditional framework for analysis of policy within a customs union is trade creation and diversion. This framework is set out and discussed in section 4.2, and its application to completion of the internal market is illustrated. The analysis provided by this approach is incomplete, because the model assumes an economic environment of perfectly competitive markets. Much of the debate on completion of the market is concerned with the effects of completion on competition, on firm size and on returns to scale. New theories of intra-industry trade capture these effects. Sections 4.3 and 4.4 are devoted to using the framework provided by these theories to analyse completion of the market.

The framework provided by models of intra-industry trade under imperfect competition permits us to analyse not only the effect of removal of trade barriers, but also the effect of moving from segmented to integrated markets. However, as has already been noted, great uncertainty attaches to the extent to which 1992 will remove market segmentation. Analysis therefore proceeds in two stages. In section 4.3 we concentrate on analysing the effects of reducing the private and social costs of trade, holding constant the degree of market segmentation. Section 4.4 adds to this the possibility that completion of market brings about complete integration of national markets and the creation of a single European market.

Section 4.5 discusses external trade policy implications of completion of the market, and section 4.6 offers some concluding comments. It should be noted that the emphasis throughout this chapter is on trade in goods. Trade in financial services is discussed in Chapter 6 of this volume.

4.1 THE REMOVAL OF TRADE BARRIERS

The main barriers to trade identified in the 1992 programme are frontier formalities, differences in technical standards, freight transport regulations and public procurement policies, together with a variety of legal trade restrictions. Our starting point is to assess the significance of these barriers, and the Community's policy to their removal. In making this assessment we need to measure three things: the private cost or 'tariff equivalence' of trade barriers, the resource cost of the barriers, and the extent to which barriers enable firms to segment markets.

4.1.1 Frontier formalities

National intra-Community frontier controls are at present retained for purposes of the administration of taxation, enforcement of legal trade restrictions, collection of statistics, and enforcement of national regulations on health, safety and police matters. The White Paper proposes 'to do away with internal frontier controls in their entirety' (para. 27). Some of their functions cease to exist as other parts of the completion programme take effect. Other functions will be passed to other agencies (for example, tax administration: see Chapter 5). Police and security matters are to be handled at the Community's external frontiers.

What is the magnitude of these barriers and the significance of their removal? To measure the tariff equivalent of frontier formalities we need to know the cost to firms of the formalities. A survey of firms conducted by Ernst and Whinney and reported in *The European Economy* (1988) estimates that administrative cost to firms of customs formalities amounts to approximately 7.5 billion ECU per annum, and in addition, delays of road haulage at frontiers costs 0.4 to 0.8 billion ECU per annum. Expressing this as a proportion of the total value of intra-Community trade we find that frontier formalities have a tariff equivalent 1.5–1.6 per cent. In addition, to the extent that administrative functions are not merely passed to other agencies, abolition of frontiers will save public administrative costs; these have been estimated to amount to between 0.5 and 1 billion ECU per

annum (Ernst and Whinney, 19). These cost savings are all resource
cost savings, and their sum is in the range 8.4–9.3 billion ECU per
annum, or some 1.6–1.7 per cent of the total value of intra-
Community trade. Other estimates have placed the resource cost
savings associated with removal of frontier controls somewhat
higher; for example, Pelkmans and Winters (1987) suggest that they
amount to at least 1 per cent and perhaps as much as 3 per cent of the
value of trade.

4.1.2 Technical standards

Industrialists perceive that variations in national product regulations
and standards constitute the most important single obstacle to intra-
Community trade (see the survey by Nerb reported in *The European
Economy* (1988)). Such barriers include legal, health and safety
regulations as well as different voluntary product standards (as set
out by the British Standards Institute, for example). The Community's approach to reducing the barriers created by these variations in standards is three-pronged. First, the process of
harmonisation of national technical regulations is to continue,
although it is recognised that this is slow and cumbersome. Second, it
is proposed to extend the existing mutual recognition principle 'that
goods lawfully manufactured and marketed in one Member State
must be allowed free entry into other Member States' (White Paper,
para. 77). Third, it is intended to expand the role of European
standardisation bodies, such as CEN (Comité Européen des Normes). These can set standards and undertake testing on a European
basis, particularly for new products for which technical specifications
have to be developed.

Reducing national variations in technical standards should save
costs by reducing the need for products to be retested and recertified
in different member countries, and by reducing the need for products
to be tailored to different specifications. The magnitude of the cost
savings vary greatly from industry to industry, and are difficult to
quantify. Industry case studies reported in *The European Economy*
provide some evidence. In the pharmaceutical industry it was estimated that multiple certification of products imposed costs on firms
of 60–80 million ECU per annum; expressing this as a proportion of
intra-Community trade in pharmaceuticals gives a tariff equivalent of
between 4 and 7 per cent. A substantial part of this also counts as
resource cost, although not all, as some of the private cost is due to

delays shortening the effective patent life during which the firm has monopoly power. In the building products industry costs of technical certification are reported to exceed costs of frontier formalities, while in the textile industry, barriers created by standards and regulations are reported to be negligible.

4.1.3 Freight transport regulation

At present intra-Community freight transport is subject to tight national regulations of two main types. The first involves the issue of a limited number of permits to intra-Community road hauliers. These permits amount to a quota system on the number of hauliers who can cross various borders, and evidence on the black market price of the permits suggest that their number is set at quite a restrictive level. Second, there is a general prohibition on 'cabotage', the use of a foreign haulier to make deliveries between two points within a country.

The Community intends by 1992 to remove entirely the system of international permits, and to secure freedom of cabotage. The reduction in average haulage prices following from this liberalisation has been estimated at an average of 5 per cent, an amount equal to around 0.1–0.2 per cent of the total value of trade, i.e. the removal of an average tariff equivalent of this size. Only part of this reduction in haulage charges is a resource cost reduction, as abolition of permits will have the effect of reducing the profits of hauliers fortunate enough to hold the permits. However, some resource cost savings will accrue. For example, it has been estimated (*The European Economy*, (1988) p. 97) that the cost of moving empty vehicles amounts to some 1.2 billion ECU per annum, and some 20 per cent of these empty moves may be due to regulatory restriction. Abolition of these restrictions would then have a resource cost saving equal to 0.05 per cent of the value of intra-Community trade. These estimates are very small compared to those obtained from a study of deregulation of the US trucking industry, which give estimates of cost savings amounting to 10 per cent of total trucking industry costs (*The European Economy*, p. 97).

4.1.4 Public procurement policies

The purchase of goods and services by government and public enterprises amounts to some 15 per cent of EC GDP. This is an area of economic life in which something close to autarky prevails, with only 2 per cent of public contracts awarded to firms from other member states. In part this is because of the product mix of public procure- ment, of which services, building and construction comprise 50 per cent. However, even controlling for product mix, there is consider- able evidence that the import content of public procurement is well below that for the private sector. This is because member states violate existing directives on the advertisement and award of con- tracts; (for example, only one quarter of the tenders which are required to be advertised in the *Official Journal of the European Community* are actually advertised). It is proposed both to tighten up enforcement of existing directives, and to introduce further directives to increase the transparency of public procurement procedures, and thereby ensure that the major part of public supply should be fully open to foreign suppliers.

4.1.5   Legal trade restrictions

In addition to the obstacles to trade sketched out above there are a large variety of other restrictions, frequently prohibiting trade in various goods or services. Article 115 of the Treaty of Rome restricts free movement within the Community of extra-Community imports against which there are national import restrictions. Thus various national voluntary export restraint agreements (notably in motor cars), and agreements such as the Multifibre Arrangement of the GATT are maintained by restrictions on movements of imported cars and textiles within the Community. Trade in banking services is in some countries limited by direct restrictions on the number and locations of branches that foreign banks can establish (see Chapter 7).

This brief and not exhaustive summary of the proposed policy changes suggests that completion of the internal market should reduce the cost of trade by an average amount equal to at least 1.6 per cent of the value of trade. Including the benefits of reduced technical barriers and transport cost savings the reductions in tariff equivalents (the trade costs imposed on firms) may be significantly greater than this. In addition, the policies seem likely to reduce firms' ability to segment markets. Certain types of transactions, notably those involving public procurement, will become more open to trade and to foreign competition. Freer circulation of goods is likely to result from the mutual recognition principle and the abolition of Article 115 controls. Combined with reduced tariff equivalents, these

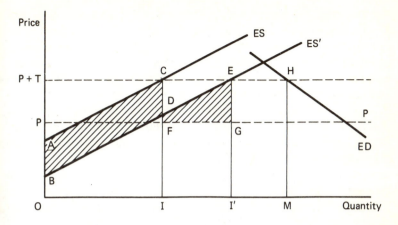

Figure 4.1   Perfectly competitive conditions.

changes should reduce firms' ability to price discriminate between markets, and should therefore force competition onto a more European-wide basis.

   Given these estimates of the direct effect of the policy, we are now in a position to do some trade theory, and analyse the indirect effects of the policy on production, trade and welfare.

4.2   TRADE DIVERSION AND CREATION

In addition to its direct benefits, trade liberalisation should improve economic efficiency as it removes barriers which cause prices, and hence consumers' and producers' marginal valuations of goods, to differ across countries. However, we know from the traditional theory of customs unions that a reduction in intra-Community barriers, given that barriers remain on extra-Community trade, may not be beneficial. There is trade diversion as well as trade creation.

   To explore these possibilities consider a model in which markets are assumed to be perfectly competitive, so that the supply curve gives the marginal cost of production as a function of output. Figure 4.1 illustrates an economy which imports a good from two sources, other European Community countries and the rest of the world. Curve ED gives the country's demand for imports of the good (demand for the good minus domestic production). ES is the supply of exports of this good from the rest of the community, and PP is the supply schedule of exports from the rest of the world. Initially assume this is perfectly elastic, so the world price is a constant, P. These imports are subject to the common external tariff of the Community, raising their price within the Community to P + T. At this price the country under consideration imports quantity OM of the product, OI coming from other member states, and IM in the form of imports from outside the Community.

Now consider a reduction in the cost of intra-Community trade, as described in section 4.1 above. This shifts the intra-Community import supply function downwards by an amount equal to the reduction in trade costs, and is illustrated on Figure 4.1 by the line ES′. Intra-Community trade now rises to OI′ and imports from outside the Community fall to I′M. Notice that, as long as the country under consideration is still importing the good from the rest of the world, its price is unchanged at P + T, and total imports are unchanged at OM. What are the costs and benefits, to the Community as a whole, of this change? The quantity of imports which were originally traded within the Community receive the direct cost savings described in section 4.1 and represented by the area ABCD. Quantity I′I of imports are now imported from other Community members rather than from the rest of the world. The cost of these are given by the area under ES′, i.e. DEI′I; before the change they were imported at world price P, and total cost FGI′I. The area DEFG is therefore a welfare reduction caused by the policy. Trade has been diverted from the lower cost producer (the rest of the world) to higher cost Community suppliers. The total benefits from the change, ABCD − DEFG, are less than the direct cost savings alone.

This example illustrates the possibility of trade diversion, but has no trade creation. Trade creation arises if the policy reduces the price of the product in the country under consideration. This can arise if either Community imports completely replace imports from the rest of the world (so the intersection of ES′ and ED is to the right of and below H on Figure 4.1), or if the rest of the world export supply schedule is less than perfectly elastic, so a reduction in imports from this source reduces the world price. This latter possibility is illustrated in Figure 4.2. Curves ES, ES′ and ED are as in Figure 4.1. The reduction in quantity of imports from the rest of the world now reduces the price at which these are imported from P to P′ (so the common external tariff inclusive price falls from P + T to P′ + T). In addition to the increase in intra-Community trade from OI to OI′ there is also now an increase in overall imports from OM to OM′.

The costs and benefits of the policy change can now be itemised as

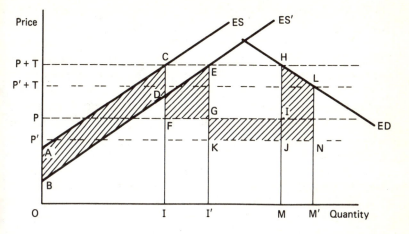

Figure 4.2   Less than perfectly elastic supply conditions.

follows. The direct cost saving from the policy is the area ABCD. Trade diversion is DEFG. Quantity I'M of imports were originally and are still imported from the rest of the world, but their price has fallen; the terms of trade gain is GIJK. Quantity MM' of trade has been created. The marginal value of these imports is given by the demand schedule, ED, and their cost to the Community by the new world price P'. The gain from trade creation is therefore the area HLNJ. The total benefit is therefore the direct cost saving, ABCD, and indirect effects, HLNJ + GIJK − DEFG. The sign of these indirect effects could be either positive or negative.

This model can be used to quantify the possible effects of completion of the market, given knowledge of the initial quantities traded, the size of the direct cost saving, and elasticities of the relevant supply and demand schedules. A study which undertakes this task for all final goods and all Community countries is Crawley and Davenport (reported in *The European Economy*). The following draws upon and presents a simplified version of the exercise they undertook, but does not report all their results. In the industries Crawley and Davenport studied, 39 per cent of Community imports were from other member states and the remainder from the rest of the world. Their method and results may be illustrated as follows. Take initial intra-Community imports as the base, so distance OI in Figure 4.2 equals 100, giving IM = 155 (OI/OM = 0.39). Crawley and Davenport take as the direct effect of the policy the Ernst and

Whinney estimates of the cost saving associated with removal of
frontier controls; these are given for each industry, and average 1.6
per cent of initial intra-Community trade, as was noted in section 4.1
above. (cf. The European Economy (1988). Given estimates of the
elasticities of the supply and demand schedules for each commodity
and for each country, the new prices and quantities can be computed.
Aggregating over countries and commodities, total intra-Community
trade rises by 3.7 per cent, i.e. $OI' = 103.7$, while imports from the
rest of the world fall by 2.2 per cent so $I'M' = 151.6$. This fall in
imports is associated with a 0.54 per cent fall in their price, as rest of
the world exporters move down their supply curves. The average
value of the common external tariff on these changes in extra-
Community imports is approximately 6 per cent.

The direct and indirect welfare effects of the policy, expressed as a
percentage of initial intra-Community trade, may now be computed
as follows:

	Direct cost saving	ABCD	=	$100.0 \times 1.6\%$	= 1.6
	Terms of trade	GIJK	=	$151.3 \times 0.54\%$	= 0.818
	Trade creation	HLNJ	=	$0.3 \times 6.0\%$	= 0.018
minus	Trade diversion	DEGF	=	$3.7 \times 6.0\%$	= 0.222

Net benefit = 2.214% of the value of
initial intra-Community
trade

We learn two things from this study. First, volumes of trade are
predicted to change in the direction one would expect but by rather
modest amounts. For the industries studied, the average increase in
intra-Community imports is 3.7 per cent and in none of the industries
studied is this increase greater than 8 per cent. The Community's
imports from the rest of the world fall, by an average of 2.2 per cent
and in no industry by more than 8.5 per cent. Second, despite trade
diversion effects, the indirect effects of completion of the market on
Community welfare are positive, and the ratio of total welfare gains
to direct cost saving is 1.38 (= 2.214/1.6). The total welfare gain is,
however, very modest, amounting to 2.2 per cent of initial intra-
Community trade, or approximately 0.2 per cent of the value of EC
consumption in the industries studied.

4.3 INCREASING RETURNS TO SCALE AND IMPERFECT COMPETITION

The preceding analysis captures the effects of trade liberalisation within a customs union as analysed by 'traditional' trade theory. However, the description it offers of the implications of completing the internal market seems incomplete. The analysis is based on perfectly competitive markets, yet competition in many European industries is far from perfect. Furthermore, it assumes constant returns to scale, while, in some industries at least, there is evidence of unexploited economies of scale. If we take these facts into account, how does it change our assessment of the effects of completion of the market?

A reduction in barriers to trade must now be thought of as reduction in barriers to competition between firms located in different countries. The effects of this are twofold. First, it increases competition in each market. This increase in competition might be expected to benefit consumers by reducing prices, and also, perhaps, by increasing the variety of products available for consumption. Second, the increase in competition tends to reduce profits and makes survival in the industry more difficult. We would therefore expect to see a reduction in the number of firms in the industry, this occurring either through exit or merger. Remaining firms are larger, so, if they have increasing returns to scale, operate at lower unit production costs. Completion of the market may therefore lead to an outcome where there are fewer and larger firms operating in Europe than at present, yet markets are also more competitive because of increased trade levels and increased import competition.

A study which quantified these effects was undertaken by Smith and Venables (1988). The approach they adopted was to construct a formal model of intra-industry trade, and then use the model to simulate the effects of completion of the internal market in a number of industries. The model they develop has the following features. First, it incorporates imperfect competition, so that firms set price in excess of marginal cost. There are many different theories of behaviour in imperfectly competitive markets, and Smith and Venables explore the cases of both price and quantity competition. The results reported here are all derived for quantity competition, i.e. under the assumption that firms are Cournot competitors. This means that each firm's mark-up of price over marginal cost is an increasing function of the firm's market share. The extreme cases of this are perfect

Table 4.1   Welfare effects of a reduction in trade costs within the EC

	EC welfare change as a % of consumption		EC total welfare change /direct cost saving	
	Short run	Long run	Short run	Long run
Footwear	0.35%	0.37%	1.30	1.37
Carpets, linoleum, etc.	0.67%	0.74%	1.43	1.57
Machine tools	0.84%	0.82%	1.50	1.46
Office machinery	0.88%	1.31%	1.49	2.22
Artificial and synthetic fibres	0.99%	1.17%	1.09	1.29
Electrical household appliances	0.64%	0.70%	1.31	1.43
Electric motors, generators, etc.	0.29%	0.29%	1.32	1.32
Motor vehicles	0.83%	0.95%	1.34	1.53
Pharmaceutical products	0.29%	0.29%	1.16	1.16

NB: Trade costs reduced by 2.5 per cent of the value of trade.

Source: Smith and Venables (1988).

competition and monopoly when firms have market shares which are infinitely small and unity respectively. All the industries studied turn out to lie in between these extremes, with mark-ups being larger the more concentrated are the industries.

The second feature of the model is the assumption that, prior to 1992, markets are internationally segmented. This means that firms are able to set different prices in different countries, and that the market shares which are used in a firm's pricing decisions are shares in separate national markets, rather than the firm's share in the EC as a whole, or in the world as a whole. A consequence of these assumptions is that firms are able to set prices relatively high in countries where they have a relatively high market share and therefore a good deal of monopoly power. The model divides the world up into six of these segmented markets, namely France, Germany, Italy, the UK, the rest of the EC and the rest of the world. Each country has a number of firms located in it, and each of these firms chooses the quantities it wishes to sell in each country, i.e. it chooses its domestic sales and its sales in each of its export markets. There is therefore intra-industry trade between countries. The model was applied to a number of industries (for listing see Table 4.1) using industry data on concentration, economies of scale and demand elasticities, and on production, consumption and trade.

The first experiment undertaken was to suppose that completion of the market implies a reduction in the direct cost of intra-Community trade. The size of the cost reduction taken was 2.5 per cent of the value of trade – somewhat greater than the direct cost of removal of frontier controls, in order to capture cost savings associated with removal of technical barriers. Some of the results of this experiment are reported in Table 4.1. Consider first the short-run effects of the reduction in barriers, where by short run we mean that the number of firms in each country is held constant although each firm may change size. The effect of the policy is to increase the volume of intra-industry trade, and by a quite significant amount, typically around 20 per cent. Increased import penetration increases competition in each market, so reducing prices and bringing gains to consumers but a reduction in firms' profits. Consumers' gains are generally around four times larger than the reduction in profits. The welfare change reported in Table 4.1 is the sum of the change in consumer welfare and firms' profits, for the EC as a whole, expressed as a percentage of EC consumption of the industries' product. As is apparent, in none of the industries we examined does the welfare gain exceed 1 per cent of the value of consumption.

In the short run the number of firms is held constant, and profits fall. In the long run the number of firms in the industry are permitted to change until profits are restored to their initial levels. This leads to a reduction in the number of firms in each industry. Remaining firms operate at a larger scale, and there are reductions in average costs of around 2 per cent in industries where returns to scale are significant, and less in other industries. The achievement of these economies of scale means that the total welfare gains are larger in the long run than in the short run, as is indicated in the long-run column of Table 4.1. However, the gains remain rather modest, in no case reaching 2 per cent of the value of consumption.

Table 4.1 also presents the total welfare gain as a proportion of the direct cost saving. This ratio exceeds unity in all cases, and is larger in the long run than in the short run. These ratios are of similar magnitude to that derived in the trade creation and diversion excercise of section 4.2 (where the ratio of total benefit to direct cost saving equalled 1.38). Gains are now coming from a different source – industrial reorganisation rather than external terms of trade improvement – but the gains remain quite small.

4.4 MARKET INTEGRATION

The preceding section presented a model which captures the interaction between economies of scale and the degree of competition in a market. However, the policy experiment described was a very conservative interpretation of what is meant by completing the internal market in that it maintained the assumption of segmented markets. As we saw in section 4.1 it is possible that completion of the market may mean a significantly freer circulation of goods within the Community, reducing the ability of firms to price discriminate between markets. The limit of this process is a situation in which markets for each product are fully integrated; firms then become players in this single market, rather than in a series of separate, segmented national markets.

The effects of switching from segmented to integrated markets were also studied by Smith and Venables (1988) using the model outlined in the previous section. The formal representation of this experiment in their model is as follows. Prior to completion of the market firms are able to set different prices in each market that they supply. After completion this ability to price discriminate is removed, and firms set the same price, net of transport costs, in all European markets. The key to understanding this second experiment is to recall that firms' market power (that is, the extent to which they mark price up on marginal cost) is a function of their market share. In the initial segmented market situation, the relevant market shares are firms' shares in each national market separately. Once markets are integrated, the relevant shares are firms' shares in the EC as a whole.

The results of switching from segmented to integrated markets, and reducing the cost of trade by 2.5 per cent, are reported in Table 4.2. For the industries in the sample which are relatively unconcentrated, for example footwear, carpets and machine tools, the difference between the experiments reported in Tables 4.1 and 4.2 is small. This is because the difference between having a market share of, say, 1 per cent of a single market, or 0.1 per cent of a unified market is trivial in terms of the amount of market power derived from such small market shares. However, for industries which are highly concentrated, the difference between the two experiments is much larger. The reason for this is that for these industries market integration is strongly pro-competitive. The difference between having a 15 per cent share in your domestic market, or just a 3 per cent share in the unified market, is a very significant loss of market power.

Table 4.2   Welfare effects of a reduction in trade costs, and of 'integration' of EC markets

	EC welfare change as a % of consumption		EC total welfare change /direct cost saving	
	Short run	Long run	Short run	Long run
Footwear	0.46%	0.50%	1.70	1.85
Carpets, linoleum, etc.	0.75%	0.75%	1.60	1.60
Machine tools	0.86%	0.83%	1.54	1.48
Office machinery	3.88%	4.10%	6.58	6.95
Artificial and synthetic fibres	4.14%	5.57%	4.55	6.12
Electrical household appliances	1.79%	2.28%	3.65	4.65
Electric motors, generators, etc.	0.52%	0.40%	2.36	1.82
Motor vehicles	4.09%	4.50%	6.60	7.26
Pharmaceutical products	1.11%	1.15%	4.44	4.60

NB: Reduction in trade costs equal to 2.5 per cent value of trade *plus* full integration of EC markets.

Source: Smith and Venables (1988).

Essentially, when markets are segmented firms are able to exploit market power over relatively captive domestic consumers. When markets are integrated, this power is simply abolished. The effects of this are to produce, in the short run, much larger consumer welfare gains and reductions in profit. Taking the electrical household appliance industry as an example, consumers gain by an amount equal to nearly 4 per cent of total consumption, and profits are reduced by 2 per cent of total consumption, giving the net welfare change of 1.79 per cent of consumption, nearly three times the net gain from a reduction in trade barriers alone (Table 4.1). In the long run, the reduction in profits leads to exit from the industry, and surviving firms are more than 30 per cent larger than before the experiment. Average costs fall significantly, and the net welfare gain rises to more than 2 per cent of consumption. Across all industries studied, we now see welfare gains reaching an average of around 3 per cent of the value of consumption, and total benefits exceeding direct cost savings by an average factor of four.

The model was also used to investigate the effects of completion on separate countries, as well as on the EC as a whole. The welfare gains from completion turn out to be quite evenly spread across countries, with no country lying far away from the EC average gains reported in the tables. For some of the industries which were studied (e.g. pharmaceuticals, footwear, electric motors) the redistribution of output between countries is also very small; some countries experience output growth and no country experiences a reduction in output of more than 2 or 3 per cent. For some other industries the changes are much larger. For example, in the integrated market experiment, for three of the industries studied there is some country which experiences a fall in output of more than 20 per cent (artificial fibres in Germany, machine tools in the rest of the EC, carpets in France). However, caution is needed in the interpretation of these results. It is possible to be relatively confident about the change in competition caused by the policy, and hence about the long-run change in firm size and the number of firms in the EC as a whole. It is more difficult to assign the exit and entry of firms to particular countries, particularly in the integrated market case where the entire definition of a country becomes somewhat tenuous.

Analysis of these different economic models suggests that the economic gains to be derived simply from reducing the cost of trade are quite small. In both the perfectly competitive model of section 4.2 and the imperfect competition model of section 4.3 economic adjustment generates total benefits which exceed the direct cost savings of the policy, but the ratio of total to direct benefit is generally below 1.5. However, the gains are very much larger if completion of the market means not just a reduction in frontier costs, but in addition, the elimination of firms' ability to segment markets, as examined in this section. The ratio of total benefit to direct cost saving then rises to over 6 in three of the nine industries studied by Smith and Venables (1988).

4.5 EXTERNAL TRADE POLICY

So far we have concentrated on the implications of 1992 for the internal trade of the EC. However, it is clear that completion of the market will also have implications for the external trade policy of the EC. Indeed, there is considerable worry outside Europe about the possibility of 1992 leading to a protectionist 'Fortress Europe'. There are several aspects to this.

First, in so far as the EC experiences a terms of trade improvement from 1992, the rest of the world experiences a terms of trade deterioration. The trade creation/diversion experiment suggests that the price of extra-community imports might fall by approximately 0.5 per cent (see section 4.2). The simulations reported in sections 4.3 and 4.4 suggest that completion of the internal market will improve the external trade position of the industries studied, this improvement coming from two sources. As intra-Community imports become cheaper, so expenditure is diverted towards these imports at the expense of imports from outside the Community. In addition, as EC firms expand, so there may be a reduction in their marginal costs which will improve the competitiveness of European firms in world markets. Once general equilibrium effects are taken into account, this improved trade position is likely to lead to appreciation of Community exchange rates against those of the rest of the world, so creating terms of trade improvement for the EC. Although other countries will lose from these terms of trade effects it would be wrong for non-Europeans to regard the change as signalling 'Fortress Europe'. All sorts of economic change have relative price effects, and such price changes do no require any policy response.

The second aspect of external trade policy concerns the fact that management of this policy now operates at the EC level (rather than the national level), and recent years have seen increasingly vigorous use by the EC of measures such as anti-dumping duties. These are legal under GATT rules, but there is fear that the EC is stretching the interpretation of the international rules. For example, anti-dumping duties have been levied not only against imports from Japan, but also against Japanese products assembled in Europe but with low local content. There is concern that Japanese products assembled in the US and imported to Europe could also be subject to these duties, so creating the possibility of trade conflict between the US and the EC.

The third cause for concern about 'Fortress Europe' stems more directly from 1992. This comes from the view that benefits of liberalisation in the EC should not be extended to non-European firms without reciprocal benefits being offered by foreign countries. For example, suppose that one EC country has an agreement with the US on mutual recognition of technical standards on some product. Post-1992 the US will then be able to export this product to the entire EC through the one country with which it has the agreement. But only the one EC country will be able to export the product to the US without undergoing further technical certification. Negotiations are needed to ensure 'reciprocity' in situations such as this.

More controversy surrounds the reciprocity principle where it might be applied in areas not covered by the GATT such as financial services. At its most extreme, it has been suggested that US banks should not be allowed access to the full European market because US interstate banking regulations restrict nationwide operations of European and US banks in the US. Furthermore, it has been suggested that this should be applied to US banks already operating in European countries, unless reciprocal access is granted in the US. If such positions were to be maintained by the EC it seems clear that trade conflict would be increased. The hope is that this can be avoided by broadening the range of the GATT. Liberalised market access in financial services could then be secured through multilateral discussions in the GATT, rather than through bilateral 'reciprocity' deals.

A further external trade policy issue faced by the EC arises from the requirement that goods circulate freely within the EC after 1992. As we have already seen, article 115 of the Treaty of Rome restricts the free circulation of goods inside the EC in support of national trade restrictions. Completion of the market requires repeal of Article 115, and hence the uniformity of external trade policy. This already applies for tariffs, but not for other import restrictions, notably quotas administered by the Multi-Fibre Arrangement, and voluntary export restraints on cars (France, Italy, UK, Spain) and other goods (e.g. consumer electronics to France). Policy on these issues is not yet formulated, but there is a real danger that existing national restrictions might be consolidated into EC-wide restrictions. These would have welfare costs for the EC (see, for example, Digby, Smith and Venables (1988) on the costs of VERs in the car industry). They would also run the risk of being seen as signals of intent to construct a protectionist 'Fortress Europe'. The external trade of the EC exceeds its internal trade, and it is important that the benefits that 1992 brings in terms of trade creation and increased competition should not be lost by trade diversion and by insulation from external competition.

4.6   CONCLUDING COMMENTS

In this chapter we have discussed how international trade theory can be used to analyse the possible effects of completion of the internal market. The insights of theory based on perfectly competitive market structures reminds us that trade diversion is possible as well as trade creation. However, a quantitative study using this analytical framework suggests that trade creation outweighs trade diversion, so that 1992 will bring economic benefits in excess of the direct cost savings it secures (section 4.2). Incorporating imperfect competition into models of trade captures the possible effects of completion of the market on the interaction between competition and scale. Studies demonstrate how 1992 may be expected to increase competition, increase the size of firms, and, in industries where there are increasing returns to scale, reduce unit costs. Once again, this suggests that the total gains from 1992 should exceed the direct effects of the policies. An important policy conclusion comes from this work. If 1992 means a reduction in trade costs while firms are still able to segment markets and so exploit market power in countries where they have relatively dominant positions, then the welfare gains turn out to be rather modest (section 4.3). The welfare gains only become large if 1992 brings about the creation of a truly integrated market, forcing firms to compete in a single unified market (section 4.4). There is no single policy measure which is sufficient to ensure that this will occur. However, the fact that the 1992 programme involves the concurrent implementation of so many separate policy initiatives, and has already been successful in raising business perceptions of the importance of Europe, seems to give reasons for cautious optimism.

References

Digby, C., Smith, A. and Venables, A.J. (1988) *Counting the Cost of Voluntary Export Restrictions in the European Car Market*, Discussion Paper No. 249, Centre for Economic Policy Research, London.

Commission of the European Communities (March 1988) 'The Economics of 1992', *European Economy*, Special edition, 35 pp. 1–222.

Pelkmans, J. and Winters, A. (1988) *Europe's Domestic Market*, Routledge & Kegan Paul, London.

Smith, A. and Venables, A.J. (1988) 'Completing the internal market in the European Community: some industry simulations', *European Economic Review*, Vol. 32, pp. 1501–25.

5 Tax Harmonisation
Alan Hamlin and Alistair Ulph

5.1 INTRODUCTION

Proposals for tax harmonisation form a major and contentious part of the overall proposals for the unification of European markets in 1992. The European Commission has produced detailed proposals in respect of the harmonisation of indirect taxes – particularly VAT and excise duties (Commission of the European Communities, 1987) – and there are more general commitments to the harmonisation of company taxation and income taxation (Commission of the European Communities, 1985). However, even where detailed proposals exist there is no general acceptance of those proposals by the governments of the member states. The UK government rejects the argument for harmonisation of indirect tax rates put forward by the European Commission and holds the view that the benefits associated with the operation of an integrated European market can be achieved without the reduction of national fiscal sovereignty implied by moves towards tax harmonisation. Some national governments (most notably Denmark) would face a very considerable loss of revenue if the proposals on VAT were implemented. For these and other reasons, it is still extremely doubtful that the Commission's proposals will be enacted in their present form by 1992.

What then are the proposals for tax harmonisation, and how can the arguments concerning their desirability be assessed? Summarising the proposals in respect of indirect taxation is relatively straightforward, and this will be the task of the next few paragraphs. Outlining the arguments for and against tax harmonisation and providing a framework within which these arguments can be assessed is a more demanding task, and will occupy most of the remainder of this chapter.

5.1.1 The proposals: VAT and excise duties

The proposals on the harmonisation of VAT fall into two categories: one concerned with the administration of the tax and the other concerned with the actual rates of tax. The present administrative system is based on the 'destination' principle, which means that the tax rate applicable to a particular good is determined at the point of sale rather than at the point of production. Thus, an item sold in the UK is subject to the relevant UK rate of VAT, with the revenue accruing to the UK government, regardless of whether the item was produced in the UK or not. The operation of this system involves rebating all VAT paid on goods intended for export – so that exporting any good is essentially a zero-rated activity. When the good arrives in the importing country VAT is applied again at that country's domestic rate. This system is policed by active border controls which serve two purposes. First, from the point of view of the exporting country, the border control checks that all goods that are claimed to be exported – and so qualified for rebates of VAT – are actually exported. Second, from the point of view of the importing country, the border control acts as a means of collecting tax on the imported goods.

The proposals put forward by the European Commission involve the tax authorities shifting their attention from the physical flow of goods across borders to the corresponding flows in the accounts of the exporting and importing companies. Exporting would no longer be a zero-rated activity and so would not give rise to claims for rebates, but correspondingly importers would find themselves paying prices that included an element of foreign tax. The domestic tax authority would rebate the (foreign) tax paid by importers and this would provide the basis of a claim against the foreign tax authority. At the same time the domestic tax authority would have claims made against it in respect of the tax inclusive export prices charged by domestic exporters. Each country's tax authority would keep records of the flow of exports and imports from the books of accounts of the firms involved, and these records would enter a central 'clearing house' where the appropriate transfers between countries would settle the accounts.

Alongside this proposed change in the method of levying VAT there are proposals for bringing the rates of VAT charged in the member countries into approximate harmony. The proposal here is that each country should operate a standard rate and reduced rate of VAT with agreement as to which goods and services are to be allocated to each rate. Furthermore, the actual rates of VAT imposed on each category of goods should fall within plus or minus 2½ per cent of the Community guidelines. Thus the standard rate of

Table 5.1   VAT rates in member states (% as at April 1987)

	Reduced rate(s)	Standard rate	High rate(s)
Belgium	6 and 17	19	25 and 33
Denmark	None	22	None
France	5.5 and 7	18.6	33.3
Germany	7	14	None
Greece	6	18	36
Holland	6	20	None
Ireland	10	25	None
Italy	2 and 9	18	38
Luxembourg	3 and 6	12	None
Portugal	8	16	30
Spain	6	12	33
United Kingdom	0	15	None
Commission proposal	4–9	14–20	None

Source: Commission of the European Communities (1987)

VAT should be within the range 14–20 per cent, and the reduced rate should be within the range 4–9 per cent. The contrast between this proposed rate structure and the present rate structures of the member states is illustrated in Table 5.1.

The European Commission's proposals with respect to excise duties are similar in spirit to the VAT proposals. However, in place of proposing approximate harmonisation of the relevant taxes, the Commission is proposing convergence to a perfectly harmonised structure. This is despite the fact that the dispersion of excise taxes across member states is currently much greater than the dispersion of VAT rates. Some examples of the proposed levels of excise duties and their relationship to existing duties in the member states are given in Table 5.2. Clearly, the Commission's proposals, if adopted, would imply very considerable changes in the relative prices of alcoholic drinks in most of the member states.

These proposals invite two distinct questions: 'What is the argument underlying the proposals and how should it be assessed?' and 'What would the effects of the implementation of these proposals be in the various member states?' The detailed empirical work required to address the second question is still in its infancy. We know of no study that systematically explores the impacts of the suggested reforms across the set of member states. Some work has been done on single-country studies, particularly under the auspices of the Institute for Fiscal Studies for the UK, and are reported in Lee, Pearson and

Table 5.2 Excise duties in member states (ECUs as at 1986)

	0.75 litres spirits	1 litre still wine	1 litre beer	1 litre petrol	1 litre diesel	Packet of 20 cigarettes[1]
Belgium	3.76	0.33	0.13	0.25	0.12	0.15 + 66%
Denmark	10.50	1.57	0.71	0.46	0.19	1.52 + 39%
France	3.45	0.03	0.03	0.39	0.19	0.03 + 71%
Germany	3.52	0	0.07	0.24	0.20	0.52 + 44%
Greece	0.14	0	0.10	0.42	0.12	0.01 + 58%
Holland	3.89	0.34	0.23	0.29	0.08	0.24 + 54%
Ireland	8.17	2.79	1.13	0.38	0.29	1.00 + 39%
Italy	0.69	0	0.17	0.53	0.12	0.03 + 69%
Luxembourg	2.53	0.13	0.06	0.20	0.10	0.03 + 64%
Portugal	0.74	0	0.09	0.41	0.18	0.04 + 63%
Spain	0.93	0	0.03	0.20	0.03	0.01 + 35%
United Kingdom	7.45	1.54	0.68	0.31	0.26	0.96 + 34%
Commission proposal	3.81	0.17	0.17	0.34	0.18	0.39 + 52–54%

[1] For cigarettes, the figures shown refer to the specific excise tax in ECUs per packet, and the ad valorem excise tax combined with the relevant VAT rate respectively.

Source: Commission of the European Communities (1987).

Smith (1988), Symons and Walker (1988) and Pearson and Smith (1988). Overall, these studies suggest that the UK government revenues could be expected to increase as a result of the reforms, and that this modest increase will be made up of much more significant shifts in the revenues raised from different goods. For example, considerable additional revenues are implied by imposing VAT at 4 per cent on items such as foodstuffs that are currently zero rated, whilst the reduction in the taxation of alcohol contained in the Commission's proposal implies a substantial loss in revenue.

Behind this pattern of revenue changes lies the more important pattern of changes in the levels of consumption of different goods. It is no surprise to learn that goods where taxes are increased may see reduced consumption and vice versa, but these direct effects are not the only forces at work. To understand the other forces we need to shift attention back to the first of our two questions concerning the arguments that lie behind the Commission's proposals and the appropriate method of evaluating those arguments.

5.1.2   The argument: indirect taxes and border controls

What then is the argument behind these proposals to harmonise European indirect taxes? In fact, the argument used by the European Commission is based almost entirely on the desire to reduce or eliminate physical border controls between countries within the Community (Commission of the European Communities, 1985, 1987). The interaction between border controls and the system of indirect taxation is clear enough, and has already been indicated – the present system of levying VAT and excise duties uses physical border controls to ensure the appropriate taxation of goods that are traded between countries.

Clearly then, if border controls are to be eliminated, or even substantially reduced, there must be at least some changes in the operation of the indirect tax systems of the countries involved. The Commission's proposals for the administrative reform of the VAT system can be seen as a direct attempt to remove the need for physical border controls. However, the Commission argues that the administrative reform alone would be inoperable without some degree of harmonisation of tax rates. The argument here is simply that widely different tax rates would provide an incentive to fraud that would be difficult to police in the absence of physical border controls. Essentially, firms would have an incentive to over-report imports of components from countries with higher VAT rates since such imports would give rise to a claim for a tax rebate. Clearly the incentives for such fraud disappear if tax rates are harmonised across countries, and it is this point that forms the basis of the Commission's proposals.

However, the strength of this argument is doubtful, and there may be alternative methods of policing the tax system that would allow different national tax rates without serious risk of fraud. Cnossen and Shoup (1987) and Lee, Pearson and Smith (1988) consider alternative arrangements and conclude that the threat of fraud is not a sufficient reason for the harmonisation of tax rates provided that there can be a considerable degree of cooperation between the national tax collection agencies. Of course, such cooperation may raise the costs of tax collecting and these increased costs should be accounted for in any overall evaluation of alternative policies.

Administrative reform is not the only means of reducing the need for physical border controls. An alternative would be to abandon the 'destination' principle in favour of the 'origin' principle which taxes goods at the rate applicable in the country of production regardless of where the good is to be sold. However, whilst taxation on the origin principle removes the need for border controls for tax purposes – since movements of goods once produced are irrelevant for tax purposes – it may introduce other problems.

Under the origin principle products from a low tax country may appear to be cheaper than identical products from a high tax country even if the high tax country were the more efficient producer, and this would produce a distortion in the pattern of production. For example, given that the UK currently imposes zero VAT on children's clothes whilst other European countries impose rates of up to 22 per cent, the origin principle of taxation would give Mothercare and other UK children's clothes firms an artificial advantage in European markets. Indeed, in the extreme case where producers are perfectly mobile, this advantage may imply that all producers should re-locate to the lowest tax country.

These distortions and location effects could be overcome if each country charged identical tax rates, and so the notion of the harmonisation of tax rates arises again – not directly as a means of eliminating or reducing border controls, but as a means of solving some of the problems that might be expected to arise once border controls are removed.

This type of argument simply establishes that some degree of indirect tax harmonisation might be expected to help in the process of dismantling border controls. But the argument says nothing on the subject of whether tax harmonisation is a desirable policy objective in its own right, or whether tax harmonisation is to be viewed as a cost to be offset against the other advantages of the removal of border controls. Even if it was agreed that tax harmonisation was desirable, there remains the question of what light economic analysis can shed on the form that a harmonised tax system should take.

To assess these broader issues of tax harmonisation we must consider some of the economic principles that underlie the design of tax systems, and it will be helpful to set out the argument in a number of steps. To establish some of the basic ideas we shall begin by considering how to design an indirect tax system in a single economy with no external trade (a 'closed' economy). While not addressing directly the issue of tax harmonisation, this will allow us to answer some of the questions concerning the form a harmonised set of taxes might take. To illustrate the results of this discussion we apply the analysis to the question of the setting of excise tax rates on alcohol.

We shall then extend the analysis to consider the design of indirect taxes in a federal system, where it is assumed that there is a single central tax authority but that there are a number of geographically and culturally distinct regions within that authority's jurisdiction. The question then is: to what extent would the federal tax authority want to harmonise taxes across its constituent regions? This is implicitly the framework in which much of the discussion of tax harmonisation within the EC is cast, and it sometimes becomes explicit when comparison is made between putative EC tax systems and those found in federal countries like the USA, Canada and Australia. Such analogies are not entirely appropriate, and we shall say something about how our arguments should be modified in a more realistic analysis of the EC where the member states are likely to retain considerably greater fiscal autonomy than is found in the regions within a federal system.

Although our discussion is limited to the harmonisation of indirect taxes – partly because this is the area in which policy proposals are most fully developed – much of what we say can be adapted to provide an economic framework for the evaluation of proposals for the harmonisation of taxes on personal incomes or corporations.

Finally we shall offer an overview of our arguments and an assessment of the merits of the cases for and against indirect tax harmonisation.

5.2   INDIRECT TAXES IN A SINGLE CLOSED ECONOMY

To answer the question of how a tax authority might design a system of taxation in a single closed economy, it is necessary first to say what objectives the tax authority might have in mind, and we shall consider four possible objectives. Obviously one objective is to raise revenue for the government, and we shall simply suppose that it has already been decided how much revenue the government requires. Secondly, the tax authority will wish to minimise the costs of administering the tax system, other things being equal. We shall follow the usual economist's procedure of treating these costs in a rather extreme way: it will be assumed that certain kinds of tax are simply ruled out of consideration, but those which are not excluded are costless to collect. Having decided what tax system this leads us to, we can then consider whether administrative considerations would lead us to modify the proposed set of taxes. A third objective is equity, which will require that the tax system is regarded as fair in the way it imposes taxes on different groups within the economy.

Finally the tax authority will want to consider how a tax system affects the efficiency with which resources are allocated within the economy, and there are two aspects to this. Taxes might be used to *improve* the allocation of resources by ameliorating a distortion; for example, it might be desirable to tax the production of aerosols to reduce the damage to the ozone layer caused by the release of fluorocarbons. However, we shall assume for the most part either that there are no such distortions in the economy, or that the government has other policies to deal with them. In that case the imposition of taxes will itself distort the allocation of resources in the economy, and the question arises of how to design a set of taxes to minimise the costs of such distortions. To focus on this question, we shall for the moment ignore the equity objective, by assuming that all households are identical. We shall concentrate on how taxes should be set on different goods and services, or what economists call *commodity taxes*; however, since we need to consider the overall allocation of resources, we need to allow the possibility of taxes being set on every good or service, including factors of production like labour, so our analysis includes some types of income tax, albeit very simple proportional income tax.

5.2.1 Three types of efficiency

It will be helpful to begin by spelling out more precisely what economists mean when they talk about the efficiency of resource allocation. An allocation is efficient if there is no other way of allocating the economy's resources that would make someone better off and no one worse off. Such an allocation can be achieved by the operation of perfectly competitive markets, and it is useful to analyse this by dividing the economy into two groups of agents, producers and consumers, and then considering three kinds of possible reallocations of resources: among producers, among consumers, and between producers and consumers.

An allocation will be *production efficient* if all producers face the same price for the same good, whether that be an input or output. Consider two producers using steel as an input, but the first faces a higher steel price than the second; each producer will employ steel to the point where the value of the extra output he gets from the last ton of steel used just equals the price he pays for steel. But then if we take some steel from the second producer (facing the low steel price) and give it to the first producer (facing the high steel price), the value of the output lost from the second producer will be less than the value of the output gained from the first producer, and so for the same total input of steel we have been able to reallocate resources to increase total output. This reallocation would take place automatically by cutting the price of steel faced by the first producer, and raising the price faced by the second producer until they were equal. We shall call the prices faced by producers *producer prices*.

Similarly, an allocation will be *consumption efficient* if all consumers face the same price for the same good, whether that be a good they buy or a factor of production they are selling. Consider two consumers who face the same price for a pint of beer, say £1, but consumer A pays £2 for a litre of wine while consumer B pays only £1. Consumers will arrange their spending on goods so that they are indifferent between spending an extra £1 on beer or wine; this means that while B would be indifferent between spending £1 on a pint of beer or a litre of wine (at the margin), A is indifferent between spending £1 on a pint of beer or half a litre of wine. But then we could take a litre of wine from B and give him an extra pint of beer and leave him no better or worse off, but by giving A the litre of wine we've taken from B in exchange for a pint of beer (which we give to B) we will make A better off. So we can keep the total amount of wine and beer consumed unchanged, but just reallocate it between consumers so as to make one better off and nobody worse off, and this will always be possible unless consumers face the same prices for all goods. We shall call such prices *consumer prices*.

Finally, *allocative efficiency* requires that producer prices should be the same as consumer prices. Suppose that the price a producer receives for producing washing machines is £100, while consumers have to pay £200. Then producers will only produce washing machines up to the point where it costs £100 in resources to produce an additional washing machine; so to produce more washing machines society will have to give up £100 worth of other goods for each extra washing machine produced. But consumers are willing to give up £200 worth of other goods to get more washing machines so clearly a reallocation of resources towards the expansion of production of washing machines could make everyone better off.

To summarise then, efficiency in resource allocation requires that all consumers and producers face the same prices for all goods and services. The imposition of taxes is bound to distort these conditions. How can we minimise the resulting distortions?

5.2.2 Minimising tax distortions

There are three steps to the argument. First it will always pay to ensure that the conditions for production efficiency are satisfied. To see why, suppose that we taxed the steel that went into the production of motor cars but not the steel that went into the production of washing machines. This would mean that producers of cars and washing machines faced different prices for steel, so that the conditions for production efficiency would not be met. But we could replace the tax on steel in motor cars with a tax on motor cars that left all consumers unaffected (and hence government revenue unaffected) and at the same time removed the inefficiency in production by equalising the producer prices of steel in the two industries. As we have already indicated, this equalisation of producer prices will allow output to increase, so that at least some people will be better off without anyone being worse off.

This argument shows that we do not want to impose taxes on intermediate stages of production, since we can always achieve better results by taxing only final products.

The second step of the argument is that, with identical consumers there can be no case for discriminating between consumers, so the

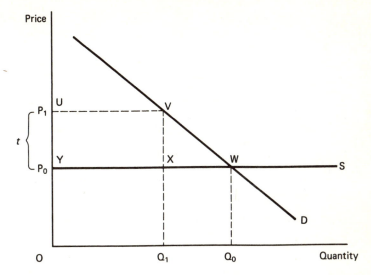

Figure 5.1   The efficiency cost of a commodity tax.

conditions for consumption efficiency should also be satisfied and all consumers should face the same prices. Combining this with our conclusion that all producers should face the same prices means that taxes should affect only the conditions for allocative efficiency, by driving a wedge between consumer and producer prices. To appreciate how we might measure the costs of this, and hence how such costs could be minimised, consider the market for a particular good shown in Figure 5.1.

Producers can supply the good at a constant price P_0, giving the supply curve S; with a demand curve D, in the absence of tax, the price to both producers and consumers will be P_0 and the quantity produced will be Q_0. If a tax t is now levied, the producer price will remain P_0 but the consumer price will rise to $P_1 = P_0 + t$.

The equilibrium quantity will now be Q_1, and the tax will raise government revenue UVXY. The cost of the tax is that consumers who would have been willing to pay at least the producer price P_0 to get output $Q_0 - Q_1$ now have to go without. The price consumers would have been willing to pay for each such lost unit of production is measured by the demand curve, and the difference between the price consumers would have been willing to pay and the price producers would have needed to receive is a measure of the net cost to society of the lost output; the cost of the tax then is measured by the area VWX.

82   *Alan Hamlin and Alistair Ulph*

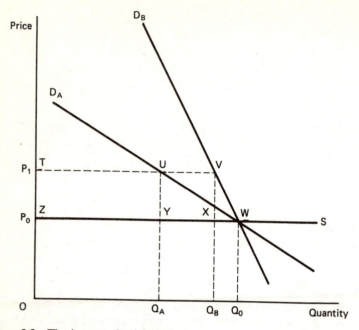

Figure 5.2   The inverse elasticity rule.

The third step of the argument then shows us how we should allocate taxes across goods to minimise efficiency costs. Consider Figure 5.2 where we show the supply and demand curves for two goods, A and B; we can suppose that both goods have the same supply price P_0, so that S indicates the supply curve for both goods, and D_A and D_B are the demand curves for goods A and B respectively. Note that the demand curve for A is more price elastic than the demand curve for B, so that a given price change will imply a larger quantity adjustment for A than for B. In the pre-tax equilibrium both goods would have equilibrium quantity Q_0 and equilibrium price P_0. If we impose the same tax t on both goods, the tax-inclusive supply price is now P_1 and the equilibrium quantities of A and B are Q_A and Q_B respectively. It is clear that we would raise less revenue from good A than from good B (area TUYZ compared to area TVXZ) and this would be at a greater efficiency cost (area UWY compared to VWX). So it would be more efficient to raise rather more revenue from good B and rather less from good A by raising the tax on B and cutting the tax on A. This gives us our first major result for how taxes should be set. It is known as the *inverse elasticity rule*, and says that the (percentage) tax rate on goods should vary inversely with their elasticities of demand.

This result needs to be qualified in two respects. First, the above analysis assumes that the imposition of taxes in one market will have no effect on the demand for goods in other markets; in technical terms it means that there are no cross-price effects. While for some purposes this might be a useful first approximation, it is clearly important to be able to analyse more general cases where there are significant cross-price effects. It is possible to modify the analysis to take account of this, and the resulting modification to the simple inverse elasticity rule for setting taxes is known as the *Ramsey rule* for taxation. While it is beyond the scope of this text to go into details, one implication that will be of some importance in what follows and is fairly intuitive is that goods which are very close substitutes for each other (and hence have large cross-price elasticities of demand) should have very similar tax rates.

The second qualification we need to make is to drop the assumption we have made so far of identical consumers. Now in principal this may lead us to drop the requirement of consumption efficiency. It may be desirable to charge a higher price for a good to rich people than is charged for the same good to poor people. It is often assumed that it is impossible to enforce this type of discrimination, although examples of groups like OAPs, students or nursing mothers being charged different prices for some goods are common. Nevertheless, it is necessary to take some account of equity considerations, and this will lead us to move away from the taxes implied by the Ramsey rule by raising taxes on goods on which rich people spend relatively high shares of their budgets and lowering them on goods on which poor people spend relatively large shares of their budgets.

5.2.3 Implementation

Having set out some of the principles that should guide the design of the tax system, let us say a little about problems of implementation. We have spoken of commodity taxes simply as a wedge between the price a producer receives for a good and the price a consumer pays. It makes absolutely no difference whether the tax is formally levied on the producer as the goods leave the factory or by the consumer as he buys it in the shop. The latter are often referred to as *excise* taxes. It is usually argued that it is easier to monitor goods coming out of factories than shops, simply because of the relatively smaller number of establishments involved. However, to ensure production efficiency, it is important that taxes only be paid by households, so simply imposing a tax on the total output leaving a factory would be inadequate unless one also ensured that where that output was used as an input at some other stage of production the tax could be rebated. This is precisely what a *value added tax* system achieves. However, a VAT system does have a slight drawback in cases where there is a significant amount of joint production; costs of administration will be lower if firms can apply a common tax rate to all their activities, and this has led to having rather few rates of VAT applied to very broad classes of goods; but while some of the early advocates of VAT thought that uniformity of tax rates was a virtue of VAT, the analysis above shows that there is no presumption that uniformity is desirable. The combination of a few VAT tax rates combined with relatively high excise taxes on a number of goods may be as close an approximation to the desirable tax system as one can get just now, though computerised accounting systems may improve the position.

5.3   AN APPLICATION OF THE ANALYSIS TO EXCISE TAXES

After this rather long review of some basic principles of tax design we can now apply the ideas we have developed to address some more practical questions. We will look at the following question: given that it has been decided to select a common set of tax rates for all member states for some set of goods, what should such tax rates be? One area where this is of particular concern is in the design of excise taxes, and, in particular excise taxes on alcoholic drinks.

One important reason for the lack of international agreement on the taxation of alcoholic drinks is that production of such drinks is undertaken by powerful national industries in many member states, and taxes are used as a protective device. Some hint of this is apparent in Table 5.2, from which it is not too hard to guess which countries are wine producers. We shall have more to say about the use of commodity taxes for protectionist purposes later. While moving to a common set of taxes would remove such protectionist practices, there remains the question of what principles should be followed in selecting that common set of taxes. We shall consider a particular case of this question – the determination of the relative rates of tax on beer, wine and spirits. Our treatment follows that of

Kay and Keen (1987) to which reference should be made for further details. Given the diversity of rates of tax on beer, wine and spirits, it might be thought that harmonisation would simply involve some political compromise between the various rates. But if harmonisation is supposed to achieve some objectives, then the rates selected should bear some relation to those objectives. We shall suppose that the objectives are those outlined at the beginning of the previous section applied at a European level, i.e. an efficient and equitable way of raising tax revenue.

The inverse elasticity rule is often invoked to argue for high rates of excise tax on alcohol and tobacco, and this might explain the high rates found in countries like the UK. It would then be necessary to assess the econometric evidence on EC-wide demand functions for beer, wine and spirits to determine the appropriate tax rates. To our knowledge such evidence has not yet been collected. However, it is not obvious on a priori grounds that the elasticities are significantly lower than on any other goods, so that it is not clear that this would justify rates higher than the highest VAT rate on other goods.

More importantly, we saw in the last section that the inverse elasticity rule depended crucially on the assumption of zero cross-price effects, and that seems particularly inappropriate in this case, for it is precisely the possibility of consumers switching between drinks that leads us to consider alcoholic drinks as a group. If it were thought that cross-price elasticities were very high (and again the econometric analysis at an EC level is not yet available) then this would lead to the important conclusion that wine, beer and spirits should all be taxed at the same rate. We shall say a little more about what that means shortly, but it is clear that this would represent quite a radical departure from the current structure. Of course, if there are other products that are significantly related to alcoholic drinks, in the sense of significant cross-price elasticities, these same considerations would apply. Estimates for cross-price elasticities between groups of products in the UK are presented and used to simulate the impact of the Commission's proposed indirect tax changes in Symons and Walker (1988).

A very different principle is that taxes on alcoholic drinks should be related to their alcohol content. Such a proposal already has support in a number of quarters, e.g. the Commission's ruling on the relative tax rates on beer and wine in the UK set tax rates which were based on the relative alcohol content of beer and an average bottle of table wine, and the Economic and Monetary Affairs Committee has also declared itself in favour of this principle. It might be argued that this is not inconsistent with the previous principle of equal tax rates on the grounds that it is the alcohol content of wine, beer and spirits that provides the basis for the high degree of substitutability between the three kinds of drink. However, this could only be defended if one believed that alcohol content was overwhelmingly the characteristic of wine, beer and spirits that determined their consumption. A little reflection suggests that this is not the case, and more significantly that it is the non-alcohol aspects of these drinks that are important in differentiating them in people's preferences. While alcohol content should be reflected in tax rates, it is not the only factor that should be taken into account.

If we accept that there is a strong case for wine, beer and spirits to be taxed at the same rate, does this mean the same ad valorem rate or specific rate? If there was a single good called wine, a single good called beer, and a single good called spirits, then it would be equal ad valorem rates, for that is how the tax formulae are calculated. Of course, for a single, homogeneous good it does not matter whether the tax rate is actually expressed in ad valorem or specific form (though ad valorem has the advantage in inflationary times of not requiring adjustment to keep real taxes constant). But the terms beer, wine and spirits each cover a very wide range of products, and while one wants to equalise ad valorem tax rates *between the product groups*, that does not imply that one also wants a constant ad valorem rate *within each product group*. The reason is that within a product group there will be a range of different qualities of product, and this will be reflected in the prices of these different products; for example, spirits differ in quality and price according to the length of time left to mature, wines will be affected by maturity, but will also depend on the weather in the particular year in which the grapes were grown. If ad valorem taxes are imposed, then better quality wines will attract a higher tax than poorer quality wines. Now in deciding what quality of goods to produce, producers will compare the price consumers are willing to pay for extra quality with the cost of producing extra quality; because ad valorem taxes rise with quality, ad valorem taxes will affect the quality of goods produced, effectively making it less economic to produce high quality goods; a specific tax, however, does not vary with quality, and so will not affect the quality of goods produced. Unless there are good reasons why one might wish to penalise higher quality products, it is more desirable if taxes within product groups are expressed in specific form.

There are two other factors that need to be mentioned. First there is the argument that a high tax on alcoholic drinks is required to reflect the cost to society of consuming alcohol (the damage to the health of the consumer, drunken driving, etc.). This is an example of the point made above that taxes may be used to correct resource misallocations. To the extent that such costs are directly related to the alcohol content of drinks (and it is not obvious that this is necessarily always the case), this would strengthen the case for taxes to bear some relation to alcohol content, though it remains true that this should not be the sole consideration.

The second factor is the equity argument for taxation. It is perhaps the case in the UK that the consumption of wine and some spirits like brandy is more prevalent among wealthier households, while consumption of beer is associated with less well off households; this would suggest a case for higher taxes on wine than on beer. Such arguments are not particularly compelling, for two reasons. First, if we are concerned with EC-wide taxation, then it is not obvious that there is any EC-wide correlation between patterns of alcohol consumption and income. Second, even if there was such a pattern it would be an average relationship which would mask a good deal of variation in alcohol consumption patterns within any income group as a result of personal preferences, religious affiliations, etc. To rely very heavily on alcohol taxation (rather than income transfers, say) to reduce inequality would leave groups like the teetotal poor disadvantaged.

Kay and Keen (1987) conclude from the above kind of analysis that if it is required to harmonise alcohol taxes the common structure should have the following properties. Beer, wine and spirits should be taxed at an ad valorem rate equal to the highest rate of VAT. The tax should be implemented through two *specific* taxes as follows. There should be a tax on the alcohol content of drinks levied on all forms of alcoholic drink at a common rate of so-many ECUs per unit of alcohol. For each product group – beer, wine and spirits – there should be a tax of so many ECUs per litre, where the tax would be different across the product groups. These two specific taxes should be levied at rates such that for the *average quality product* within each group the total tax in ad valorem terms should be equal to the highest rate of VAT. This set of proposals is rather different from any being discussed by the officials in the EC, and shows the value of applying a set of principles derived from clearly stated objectives, rather than trying simply to reach a compromise among a number of different starting positions.

5.4 COMMODITY TAXES IN A FEDERATION

Having outlined the principles that should govern the design of commodity taxes in a single, closed economy, and illustrated those principles in a particular setting, we now want to extend the analysis so as to be able to examine the principles that might lead to a case for tax harmonisation across different areas. We begin by retaining the assumption that there is a single (ultimate) tax jurisdiction, but introduce a number of distinct sub-regions within the economy. Such a structure is a type of federalism, although federal countries typically divide the powers of taxation between the central government and the regional governments and here we are assuming that tax powers all lie with the central government. The question is whether such a central authority would wish either to set regionally distinct tax rates, or, more powerfully, to actually delegate some tax-raising powers to the sub-regions. If the answer to these questions is yes, then this will tell us that there can be no presumption that tax harmonisation is a good thing in itself, and that there may be an optimal degree of variation in tax systems. Our discussion should also tell us something about the circumstances in which more variety will be desirable and the circumstances in which greater harmonisation will be desirable.

5.4.1 Production efficiency again

The first point to note is that the argument put forward in relation to the single, closed economy about the desirability of ensuring that the tax system preserves production efficiency carries over directly to the federal case. This implies that throughout the community producers should face the same set of producer prices and there should be no taxation on intermediate stages of production. The uniformity of *producer* prices is what is required to ensure that there is no attempt by any member state's government to discriminate between its domestic producers and producers in the rest of the Community. To ensure that production efficiency is achieved what is required is either a destination-based VAT system in which imports from other member states enter a country free of tax, or, equivalently, excise taxes that are levied only at the stage where goods reach households. As we argued above, it is possible to implement such systems without border controls provided one can enforce honest book-keeping.

5.4.2 Consumption efficiency again

We shall assume for the moment that all households buy their consumer goods, and supply their factors of production, in the country in which they are resident. In that case there is no reason to suppose that the rates of VAT or excise duties need to be the same between member states, for the only reason for requiring consumption efficiency is either that consumers are identical, or that it is impossible to enforce different prices for different consumers. But the assumption that there is no cross-border shopping means that it is possible to use geographical location as a basis for discriminating between consumers. And if there is any difference between the constituent regions in terms of either the distribution of income or consumer preferences (in particular the pattern of own- or cross-price elasticities of demand, or the variation in budget shares of different commodities across income groups) it will pay the tax authority to set different commodity taxes in different regions for either efficiency or equity reasons.

To return to the example of alcoholic drinks, if it was the case that in the UK beer was predominantly drunk by poorer families, while wine was drunk by better off families, that might provide a rationale for the UK charging lower taxes on beer than wine, while the reverse might be true in France. Provided there is no attempt to protect brewers in one country from competition from other EC brewers, or vineyards in one country from competition from other EC vineyards, the condition for production efficiency is met. Such a tax structure will in general alter the levels of production of beer and wine and may have the effect of raising the output of beer in the UK and reducing the output of wine in the UK, but although these effects may look as though they are evidence of the use of taxes as a means of exploiting international market power (see below), in fact they are simply the consequence of an attempt to raise tax revenue as efficiently and equitably as possible, as was illustrated in Figure 5.2 above. The point here is that an efficient and equitable tax system will carry implications for the international distribution of production, but the choice of the tax system is not motivated by a desire to favour production in any particular country.

Since differences between member states of the Community in terms of the pattern of consumer preferences or income distribution seems an eminently plausible assumption, we have reached a rather important conclusion: that tax harmonisation in a federal system should ensure the establishment of production efficiency but that any attempt to harmonise tax rates is likely to reduce either the efficiency or fairness with which tax revenue is raised.

5.4.3   Cross-border shopping

We have assumed so far that there was no cross-border shopping. This is clearly unrealistic. One interpretation of the effects of cross-border shopping is that it will make a particular commodity sold in one member state a perfect substitute for the same commodity sold in another (perhaps neighbouring) member state. Then the analysis presented above tells us that indeed it would be desirable to set equal tax rates on such goods. But it needs to be realised that this does not provide an argument for harmonisation of all taxes, for the extent to which cross-border shopping makes goods sold in different countries perfect substitutes will vary depending on the nature of the goods and the nature of the borders. At one extreme there may be goods which can be bought by mail order so that customers can purchase from another country even if they live quite far from borders. Here prices could not differ by more than postal rates (though there is also the problem of frequency of purchase and convenience). Next comes the case of genuine cross-border shopping where people living close to the border could cross over and buy in a neighbouring country. While this is likely to affect a much wider range of goods, it is likely to affect only a relatively small number of people and hence sales, so it is not clear that at the aggregate level this would make goods perfect substitutes. This would also depend upon the costs of crossing borders, so that it may be much easier for the UK to implement taxes different from those in the rest of Europe than it would be for Luxembourg simply as a matter of geography. Rather more people are likely to be involved in cross-border shopping as an indirect consequence of tourism, but this is unlikely to affect some items, such as very bulky furniture. Finally, there are non-traded goods, such as electricity, restaurant meals, etc., which can not be exported. As one moves from the first case to the last the case for harmonisation becomes successively weaker.

All of this would suggest that the Commission's plans to ensure that all commodity taxes do not vary by about more than 2.5 per cent on either side of some Community norm may be too restrictive. What one might expect would be groupings of commodities on which the band within which taxes could be varied across countries could be made narrow or broad depending on the kind of considerations outlined above. For example, there may be no need to harmonise the taxation of restaurant meals or construction at all, whilst it may be desirable to tax small, high value consumer durables such as cameras similarly in all countries.

5.4.4 Taxes as protection from international competition

However, there is an important caveat to this position. What we have shown is that if a single tax authority could set taxes in all member states it would in general wish to set regionally distinct tax rates on at least some goods. But that is not the same as allowing member states to set their own commodity taxes. For even if production efficiency is maintained by the imposition of destination-based commodity taxes, and explicit tariffs against imports are effectively ruled out, countries could still use commodity taxes as devices to exploit market power. For example, if much of UK wine consumption was imported from France and that was a significant part of French production, so that a reduction in UK consumption would reduce the producer price of French wine, then it would pay the UK to raise the tax on wine (both domestic and imported) relative to the rate that would be set by the single tax authority in order to gain the advantage of lower producer prices from France, even though this would also reduce the producer price for domestic vineyards. If all member states try to exploit their market power then, as usual in trade theory, we end up in a position where all member states are worse off than if they had renounced such policies.

These considerations clearly play an important part in the Commission's thinking, but their implications for harmonisation of tax rates are less than clear-cut. For while harmonisation eliminates the ability of countries to try to exploit market power in their trade with other member states, it also eliminates the genuine efficiency and equity gains that can be derived from differential commodity taxation across countries that would be imposed by a single EC-wide tax authority. Keen (1987) has shown that starting from a set of arbitrary commodity taxes in various member states, a move to harmonisation on the basis of an average of the pre-existing tax rates will be desirable. But he shows this in a context where the *only* role for commodity taxes is to exploit market power, so that the ideal would be the complete *elimination* of all commodity taxes. In the analysis we have been conducting (which is more pertinent to the situation actually faced in the EC) commodity taxes play a real efficiency and equity role in raising revenue, and more to the point, inter-country differences in tax rates play these roles.

5.4.5   Information requirements

The discussion so far suggests that while there is no case for aiming at harmonisation of all commodity taxes, it should not be left to individual member states to determine how far they should deviate from other countries in setting commodity taxes. This brings us to a further consideration which may go in the direction of favouring harmonisation. We have supposed that the Commission would have sufficient information about income distribution, consumer preferences, etc., in individual member states to be able to work out an optimal set of country-specific tax rates. But suppose that the Commission needs to rely on member states to provide the relevant information, then there arises the danger that member states would try to convince the Commission that there were equity or efficiency reasons for departing from an EC norm, when in fact there were no such reasons, and the only reasons were to gain trade advantages. In other words it would be impossible for the Commission to discriminate between genuine and phoney reasons for departing from some common tax structure. In this case a rule of no departures – complete harmonisation – might seem attractive.

But this seems rather far-fetched. Unless the Commission is just going to settle for a crude political compromise in which it sets a common set of taxes as an average of the existing taxes in member states (which we said in the last section was an undesirable way to approach the problem), then it is going to have to gather data on consumption patterns etc. across member states. The data it would need to establish a sensible set of harmonised tax rates is no different from the data it would need to determine the appropriate country-specific tax rates.

If the Commission is to have both the powers and the information to set a sensible set of harmonised taxes, those same powers and information should enable it to set country-specific taxes, and casual empiricism suggests it will be desirable to do so. This may sound as if it is giving up authority over taxation to the central European authority, but in fact it may be put in a way which makes it clear that this is not so to any great extent – certainly to a lesser extent than is implied by the present harmonisation proposals.

In essence we have argued that there may be considerable efficiency and equity gains from countries operating distinct commodity tax rate structures, but that there are other reasons why individual countries may choose commodity taxes that are essentially to do with exploiting market power over other countries. What is required is a system that allows the former type of consideration but disallows the latter. But this system need not be centralised, so that we do not need to think of the European Commission setting tax rates for each country over the heads of the national governments. Rather we could think of a system in which national governments set their own tax rates but are required to show that the pattern of taxes adopted is not motivated by the desire to exploit the gains from trade. This interpretation gives the Community only the power to object to tax policies that are adopted as offensive weapons against other members of the Community, and this may seem to be a reasonable power in the context of a voluntary community.

5.4.6 Taxation and expenditure

There is one further point that should be mentioned. In using the analogy between a federal society and the EC we have glossed over one very considerable distinction between the two cases. In the simple federal setting we have adopted all revenue accrues to the central treasury and can be allocated to expenditures in any of the constituent regions, so that there is no necessary link between the tax revenues generated in a particular region and the level of public expenditure in that region. Indeed, a major focus of attention in the literature devoted to federal tax policy is precisely the redistribution between regions or states. But in the EC context it is clear that, however the commodity taxes are set – whether by national governments with complete discretion, a central European agency, or some intermediate system involving both national and European administrations – the revenues will accrue directly to the national governments concerned, so that there will be a direct link between the tax revenues generated in each country and the levels of public expenditure.

Of course, the EC does engage in some redistribution between the member states – most obviously within the Common Agricultural

Policy and the Regional Fund – but inter-country redistribution is no part of the plan for tax harmonisation. In the absence of any such redistribution, it is clear that any move towards harmonisation of taxes must also involve a loss of flexibility in setting expenditure levels.

The point here can be seen very clearly by returning to the basic purpose of taxation – the raising of revenue. In our earlier analysis we assumed that the revenue requirements of the national government were set and that the resultant tax problem could be thought of as raising that revenue in the most equitable and least inefficient way possible. But if we are to set the same tax rates in each of several countries this will limit the ability of those countries to raise the levels of revenue that they require. You simply cannot allow each country to specify its own revenue requirement and simultaneously specify that tax rates have to be the same in each country.

This then is a further argument against full-scale tax harmonisation. It conflicts with the ability of each country to determine its own desired level of public expenditure. Of course, indirect tax rates could be harmonised whilst still allowing countries to adopt different income and corporation tax policies in order to fulfil their revenue requirements, but even this degree of harmonisation may effectively force countries to adopt income or corporation tax systems that might carry severe efficiency or equity costs, and this could only be justified if there were very substantial benefits to the harmonisation of indirect tax rates.

5.5   OVERVIEW AND CONCLUSIONS

We have spent some time laying out the nature of the arguments that underlie the choice of commodity tax rates and therefore provide the framework for evaluating harmonisation proposals. Before offering our conclusions it is worthwhile to bring together the main points of the argument in summary form.

(a) The major characteristics of a tax system on which it should be evaluated are: (i) its ability to raise required levels of revenue, (ii) its impact on the efficiency of resource allocation, and (iii) its equity.

(b) The notion of efficiency can be broken down into three parts: (i) production efficiency, which involves all producers facing the same prices, (ii) consumption efficiency, which involves all consumers facing the same prices, and (iii) allocative efficiency, which involves consumer prices being equal to producer prices.

(c) In all the circumstances we discuss production efficiency will be both desirable and achievable. This implies that there should be no taxes on intermediate products. This is achieved, for example, by a destination principle value added tax.

(d) Consumption efficiency will be desirable if all individuals are identical, but if groups of individuals differ in their preferences or their incomes, efficiency and equity gains may be available by departing from uniform consumer prices. This can justify taxes which differ between regions on a particular good in exactly the same way that it can justify peak and off-peak prices for electricity, or low rail fares for pensioners.

(e) Commodity taxes by their nature drive a wedge between producer and consumer prices and so entail inefficiencies. Minimising the inefficiency for any given tax revenue will typically involve taxing different goods at different rates. Three factors are of particular importance in determining the appropriate rate structure: (i) the price elasticity of demand for the good (other things being equal we will want to place relatively high tax rates on goods with relatively low elasticities of demand), (ii) the availability of substitutes (if two goods are good substitutes for each other they should be taxed at similar rates), (iii) the distributional characteristics of goods (goods that are consumed predominantly by the poor should be taxed at lower rates than goods consumed predominantly by the rich).

(f) Under certain conditions commodity taxes can be used as a type of hidden trade barrier that can act to the advantage of the tax-setting nation even if the cost to other countries is large. Viewing the countries together, this use of taxes will be undesirable.

This line of argument points to the following conclusions. First, the optimal set of commodity taxes seen from the European viewpoint is unlikely to involve identical tax rates in each country. The differences in consumer expenditure patterns between the member states is a good indicator that efficiency and equity gains will be available to a system that allows country-specific tax rates.

Second, the desired degree of harmonisation in tax rates will vary from product to product. Some goods are such that they are good substitutes across national boundaries, and our analysis tells us that good substitutes should be taxed similarly. But other goods are not internationally substitutable and so tax rates can diverge quite markedly if this is indicated by other considerations. For example restaurant meals in London are not good substitutes for restaurant meals in Rome (even if the food is identical) and there is no requirement that they should be taxed at similar rates (any more than there is a requirement that they should be sold at the same price).

Third, harmonisation of tax rates carries strong implications for tax revenues in the various countries – and therefore for the levels of public expenditure in each country. It may not be feasible to match a harmonised tax system with each country's legitimate expenditure plans. One possible way around this problem would be the more fully federal approach to fiscal policy which would involve explicit transfers from the tax revenues of some countries to the expenditures of others. However, even in this setting, the optimal federal tax structure would still not involve full harmonisation of commodity tax rates. In the absence of international transfers the desirable degree of harmonisation will be still less.

All of this amounts to the proposition that there is no general case for the international harmonisation of commodity tax rates. Tax rates should be allowed (indeed, encouraged) to diverge to the extent that the differences can be motivated by appeal to arguments of the type rehearsed above under the titles of efficiency and equity. But, to the extent that we take a European rather than a strictly national viewpoint, differences motivated by the desire to exploit trading partners might be a proper concern for international coordination.

How then does all of this relate to the actual proposals for indirect tax harmonisation currently on the table, and the argument used to support those proposals? First, it is clear that the proposals for VAT rate bands (Table 5.1 above) and excise duties are essentially political compromises rather than the results of any economic analysis of the type suggested here, so that the degree of harmonisation they involve (and the particular rate structure chosen) is essentially arbitrary. In the absence of detailed empirical work it is simply not possible to say whether bringing European commodity tax rates closer together will prove to be a cost or a benefit. All our argument here has done is to show that we cannot presume that it is a benefit.

It is also clear that the potential costs and benefits associated with the appropriate design of taxes may be large relative to the benefits that may be expected to flow from the reduction of physical border controls – particularly since it is difficult to imagine national governments completely abandoning such controls given their significance in areas unrelated to commodity taxes (immigration policy, drug trafficking, etc.). But it is also the case that the costs of inappropriate tax rates are diffuse and inherently difficult to quantify since they are reductions in the overall efficiency and equity of the economy, whilst the costs of maintaining physical border controls are more concentrated and directly visible. This may explain why some are willing to see harmonisation simply as a means of effecting a reduction in the costs of border controls, even though there is no real reason to link these two policies.

Overall, then, we have argued that differences in the economies of the member states provide good reasons for differences in the structure of their commodity tax rates and that harmonisation can not be viewed as a desirable goal in itself. Although our discussion has been limited to the case of commodity taxes – partly because this is the area in which the proposals for tax harmonisation are most advanced – similar economic analysis of the cases of the direct taxation of personal incomes and corporations is possible and would lead to the same general pattern of results.

References

Cnossen, S. and Shoup, C. (1987) 'Coordination of value-added taxes', in S. Cnossen (ed.), *Tax Coordination in the European Community*, Kluwer.
Commission of the European Communities (June 1985) *Completing the Internal Market*, White Paper from the Commission to the European Council.
Commission of the European Communities (1987) *Completion of the Internal Market: Approximation of Indirect Tax Rates and Harmonisation of Indirect Tax Structure. Global Communication from the Commission*, COM(87)320.
Kay, J.A. and Keen, M. (1987) 'Alcohol and tobacco taxes: criteria for harmonisation', in S. Cnossen (ed.), *Tax Coordination in the European Community*, Kluwer.
Keen, M. (1987) 'Welfare effects of commodity tax harmonisation', *Journal of Public Economics*, Vol. 33, pp. 107–14.
Lee, C., Pearson, M. and Smith S. (1988) *Fiscal Harmonisation: An Analysis of the European Commission's Proposals*, Institute for Fiscal Studies, Report No. 28.
Pearson, M. and Smith, S. (1988) '1992: issues in indirect taxation', *Fiscal Studies*, Vol. 9, pp. 25–35.
Symons, E. and Walker, I. (1988) *The Revenue and Welfare Effects of Fiscal Harmonisation for the UK*, Institute for Fiscal Studies, Working Paper No. 88/8.

6 1992 and the UK Labour Market

Martin Chalkley

6.1 INTRODUCTION AND OVERVIEW

The claimed benefits of 1992 are many. Greater consumer choice, lower prices, higher output (GNP) and faster growth are all supposed to follow from the removal of the various barriers to intra-European trade. The claims of the proponents of the 1992 reforms with respect to these benefits are critically assessed elsewhere in this volume. The purpose of the present chapter is to consider the consequences of 1992 for the UK labour market.

There would appear to be two avenues through which the approach of 1992 will have an impact upon the UK labour market. First, some specific policy proposals within the 1992 programme will directly affect labour markets within the EC. These reforms are only a very small part of the overall programme and involve moves to ensure recognition within the Community of professional qualifications together with the removal of barriers to the mobility of individuals. In certain areas of the labour market therefore there will be a move towards the establishment of 'European' as distinct from national markets for particular types of labour services – most particularly those associated with the 'professions'. The implications for the functioning of labour markets of these kinds of changes are not discussed at all in existing references.

Second, there are the indirect consequences of the removal of barriers in product markets. It is claimed that the 1992 programme will lead to a restructuring and reorganisation of production into a more efficient form. To take advantage of economies of scale some manufacturing plants must close whilst others expand. This 'rationalisation' will result in a change in the pattern of demand for labour. I shall refer to such an impact as the *structural effect*. In addition, improved efficiency and increased competition will, it is claimed, lead to lower prices and increased output. This expansion will result in greater employment. I shall refer to this as the *aggregate effect*.

Finally the reorganisation of production can be expected to affect both the regional pattern of employment opportunities and the composition of job opportunities in terms of skill requirements. This I shall refer to as the *compositional effect*.

The approach taken to these indirect consequences for European labour markets in the publications concerning 1992 has been rudimentary. There has not in fact been any discussion or estimation of the structural or compositional effects described above. In considering the aggregate effect there have been only crude estimates based upon macroeconomic models of the European economy. These provide only Europe-wide estimates of increases in employment and do not break the total down by country.

Existing literature regarding 1992 does not therefore provide either a framework for considering the likely impact of completed internal markets upon the labour market nor does it provide estimates of this impact. The tasks here are therefore to provide such a framework and where possible to quantify effects. To accomplish these tasks I shall be using a model of the functioning of labour markets that concentrates on dynamics.

In their attempts to explain more precisely the determinants of employment, wages and unemployment, economists have increasingly concentrated upon the dynamic functioning of labour markets. At any time within a labour market there is considerable activity. Currently unemployed workers are seeking jobs, firms with vacancies are seeking workers, jobs are being destroyed and created. Economic analysis that takes account of these real-world features of labour markets is far more successful in coming to terms with the secular increase in unemployment in Europe over the last decade. Indeed this increase can be decomposed into the consequences of macroeconomic fluctuations (aggregate) and structural effects. In addition it is possible to analyse the consequences of compositional change and the consequences of combining two separate labour markets into a unified whole, all within terms of the kind of dynamic model with which I shall be concerned. Such a model therefore suits the purposes of this chapter rather well.

To motivate what follows I provide at the end of this section a brief summary of the operation of the UK labour market as portrayed in published statistics. In the next section of this chapter I summarise the features of a dynamic analysis of the UK labour market which I then use to address the likely implications of the 1992 programme at three levels. In section 6.2 I look at the aggregate and structural effects of 1992. I use an empirical analysis of the UK to estimate the magnitude of these effects. Section 6.3 is then concerned with the compositional and direct effects of 1992. The analysis here is qualitative rather than quantitative. Nevertheless a number of interesting conclusions and policy recommendations can be deduced. Leading up to 1992, for example, it may be important to reconsider the role of government policy towards disadvantaged regions. In section 6.4 I briefly summarise the main arguments.

6.1.1 Overview of the UK labour market

The following data are derived from information published in the Department of Employment *Monthly Gazette*. They relate to June 1987 unless otherwise indicated.

As of June 1987 21.8 million individuals were employed by firms or other organisations, 2.8 million were self-employed whilst a further 300,000 served in the armed forces and an almost equal number were engaged in government sponsored training programmes. The UK workforce at this time (defined as being those in one of the above categories or claiming state benefits) was 28.3 million. Unemployment therefore stood at 2.9 million or 9.75 per cent of the workforce. There is and always has been controversy over the measurement of unemployment. The figure of 2.9 million understates the true reserves of employable labour in the UK as of June 1987 because some employable individuals genuinely seeking work would not have been eligible for benefits. At the same time some benefit claimants would not have accepted employment if it had been offered. Their presence therefore exaggerates true unemployment. Numerous attempts have been made to estimate true unemployment and how it deviates from the official unemployment measure. There is, however, no consensus as to how unemployment ought to be measured. The figure of 2.9 million is the one that must therefore be worked with. A breakdown of total unemployment by duration and by region within the UK is as follows:

Unemployment duration (proportion of the unemployed)

Less than 2 weeks	2–4 weeks	4–8 weeks	8–13 weeks	13–26 weeks	26–52 weeks	Over 52 weeks
0.07	0.046	0.065	0.066	0.14	0.18	0.42

Unemployment in the regions (% of regional workforce)

	SE	GL	SW	EA	WM	EM	YH	NW	N	W	S	NI
000s	680	363	178	72	305	184	286	403	213	157	345	127
%	7.1	8.2	8.3	6.8	11.3	9.2	11.6	13.0	14.3	12.8	13.3	17.8

The Regions:
SE: South East; GL: Greater London; SW: South West; WM: West
Midlands; EA: East Anglia; EM: East Midlands; YH: Yorkshire and
Humberside; NW: North West; N: North; W: Wales; S: Scotland;
NI: Northern Ireland.

Unemployment is clearly unevenly distributed over the regions.
The worst regions suffer over twice the unemployment rate of the
best. Whilst these numbers relate to a single date, the pattern that is
suggested persists over time. The North, Scotland, Wales and Northern Ireland suffer persistently high unemployment compared with the
South.

A quick glance at the duration data suggests that unemployment is
a dynamic phenomena. Of the unemployed 7 per cent had been
without a job for less than two weeks. A further 17 per cent had been
unemployed for between two weeks and three months, this at a time
when unemployment was at historically high levels. Generally unemployment is a far more short-term phenomenon than indicated by
these figures. Turnover amongst both the unemployed and filled jobs
is further indicated by the fact that in manufacturing industry at this
time approximately 2 per cent of filled jobs fell vacant during a
four-week period being matched by an almost equal percentage of
jobs being filled. To gain further insight into the idea that even at
times of high unemployment, the unemployed coexist with unfilled
jobs, we can look at vacancies as notified to job centres both
nationally and regionally:

Vacancies (000s) (as notified to regional job centres)

	UK	SE	GL	EA	SW	WM	EM	YH	NW	N	W	S	NI
V	233	87	36	8	20	21	13	16	25	12	12	18	2
V/U	0.24	0.39	0.30	0.33	0.34	0.21	0.21	0.26	0.18	0.17	0.23	0.16	0.05

The second row above reports the corrected ratio of vacancies (V)
to unemployment (U). It is thought that vacancies notified to job

centres account for only one third of all vacancies. As can be seen scaling up vacancies by a factor of three implies that in the UK at this time there was one vacancy for each four unemployed workers. Again, however, there is considerable regional dispersion which serves to reinforce the picture presented by the unemployment data. Disadvantaged regions suffer high unemployment but have fewer vacant jobs. There were eight times as many jobs per unemployed worker in the best as compared with the worst region.

The above data represent the facts about the UK labour market that need to be borne in mind when considering the likely impact of 1992. The UK labour market operates such that the identity of the unemployed and the location of unfilled jobs is continuously changing whilst the stock of unemployment and of vacancies remains high. There is considerable regional variation both in unemployment rates and the availability of vacancies.

6.2   1992 AND THE UK LABOUR MARKET: AGGREGATE AND STRUCTURAL EFFECTS

The purposes of this section are to explain how the policies that lead to the completion of the internal market may feed into the UK labour market and to go some way towards quantifying the effects. In order to achieve this I first outline a simple model of the UK labour market. Such a model helps to organise one's thinking about the way that the approach of 1992 may indirectly influence the UK labour market via structural and aggregate effects referred to in section 6.1. It is also useful in pointing to ways in which a simple summary (for example, in terms of aggregate employment) of the effects of 1992 may be misleading.

The model I consider concentrates on the determination of employment, unemployment and the level of vacancies. This reflects a change that has taken place in economists' thinking about unemployment. It is regarded as overly simplistic to regard unemployment as an ill that should be reduced at all costs. Some unemployment is good because it reflects a mechanism by which individuals relocate towards more suitable or more productive employment.

It is best to think of 'problem unemployment' as occurring when there are insufficient vacant jobs to ensure that unemployed individuals can find employment reasonably quickly. Therefore it is necessary to think carefully about what represents a beneficial (or detrimental) effect upon the labour market. I shall take it to be the case that current unemployment levels are of the 'problem' kind. A reduction in unemployment with no reduction in vacancies would therefore be beneficial as would an increase in vacancies with no increase in unemployment. In this latter case the length of time for which any one individual will remain unemployed will be shorter. In the first case employment will also be higher but as we shall see this is not necessarily true of the latter. Since these variables are central to most people's concerns about the operation of labour markets this is a convenient feature of the analysis.

6.2.1 Employment, unemployment, vacancies and wages

The general view taken of unemployment has changed considerably over the past 20 years. From being seen as evidence of some failure of the labour market to adjust, unemployment is now viewed as a reflection of a constantly adjusting labour market. Considerable evidence has been gathered as to the transitory nature of unemployment for many individuals (e.g. that analysed by Junankar and Price (1984)). At any time there exist vacancies together with unemployed individuals; these too are transitory being filled or replaced by different job opportunities. It is therefore important to distinguish between both the stock of jobs and employment and between the workforce and the employed, and to realise that in each case the latter is some changing subset of the former. It helps to use some notation. I will use E to denote the total number of individuals employed, J the total number of jobs, L the total labour force, U unemployment and V vacancies. By definition $V = J - E$ and $U = L - E$.

The dynamic nature of the labour market is reflected in the fact that the identities of the unemployed and of the jobs that are vacant are constantly changing. This leads us to consider the nature of the implied relationship between V and U. Suppose for simplicity that every month some fixed proportion of employed individuals become unemployed. This in fact turns out to be a reasonable approximation for the UK since employee (quit) and employer (layoff) initiated separations are inversely correlated (see Nickell (1982)). Suppose further that vacancies are filled in any month both according to how many unemployed there are and how many vacancies exist. This again accords well with the evidence for the UK (see Pissarides (1986)). These two facts suggest a relationship between U and V such

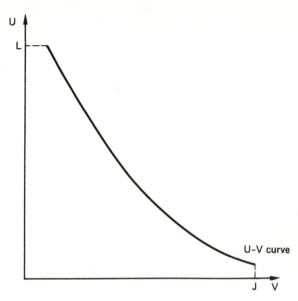

Figure 6.1   The U–V curve.

that the labour market is in a dynamic equilibrium, i.e. with U and V not changing but with turnover amongst both the unemployed and vacant jobs. The higher is unemployment the lower is employment and the smaller the flow into unemployment. If unemployment is to remain constant the lower must be the stock of vacancies. In other words a dynamic equilibrium of the labour market requires a negative relationship between U and V. Such a negative relationship is consistent with the observed levels of U and V. Indeed the U–V curve as it is often called has been the subject of much comment and attention for at least 30 years. Observation suggests that the U–V curve in fact has a shape similar to that sketched in Figure 6.1.

The U–V curve is quite a powerful tool when it comes to understanding what goes on within the labour market when outside influences change. Before elaborating the U–V curve diagram further it is perhaps worth thinking about what determines the position of the U–V curve. In Figure 6.2 suppose that we initially observe the UK labour market with unemployment U_1 and vacancies V_1. If we additionally know E and L we can draw both L and J on the diagram. Notice the necessity for the distance $J - V$ to equal the distance $L - U$. This allows us to use a 45 degree line as in Figure 6.2 to

Martin Chalkley

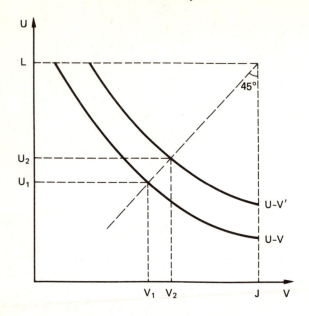

Figure 6.2   Determining the position of the U–V curve.

determine which point along the U–V curve we will actually observe
(i.e. U_1, V_1).

   Suppose now that the rate at which jobs break up increases but that
everything else were to remain unchanged. The main reason given
for a change in the rate of job break-up is so-called mismatching in
the labour market. The idea is that increased variability in the
demand for different products will cause jobs and workers to be less
easily matched. If this happens, then for employment $L - U$ to be
sustained vacancies must be filled at a faster rate. For this to be the
case there must be more unemployed workers, more vacancies or
both. In other words the U–V curve is shifted to the right to something like U–V'. Of course U_1, V_1 cannot be an equilibrium in a
labour market with U–V'. In fact we would need to move to the point
U_2, V_2. A second set of factors thought to affect the position of the
U–V curve are the decisions of the unemployed workers. If either the
general willingness of unemployed workers to accept employment or
the intensity with which job offers are solicited decrease, we should
expect the U–V curve to shift to the right. For this reason there have
been attempts to explain increases in the observed level of unemployment by reference to the increased generosity of unemployment

benefits. The U–V curve gives us some idea of the kind of measures that might be useful in reducing unemployment. It is not, however, the whole story. Before we can distinguish between various kinds of policy towards the labour market we need to consider what it is that determines the actual point along the U–V curve to which the market tends.

There are two elements missing in the analysis considered so far. First there is no discussion of the decisions of firms in the economy which create jobs. Second, and largely tied up with the first deficiency, there is no discussion of wage determination. To remedy these deficiencies, we may start by thinking about the determinants of the number of jobs J. The conventional analysis of the demand for labour stresses a number of influences that should be important in determining J. Firms will wish to employ more individuals the lower are wages, the more productive is labour and the more valuable is labour's product (i.e. the higher is the price of output). It is also generally thought that employment will be higher the lower are other costs of producing output although this is not clear since it may be more profitable to replace labour with the now cheaper alternative inputs. I shall take it to be the case that J responds as indicated above to these various influences. The number of jobs in fact ties down the equilibrium of the labour market under consideration. To see this consider Figure 6.3.

If, as in Figure 6.3, the number of jobs increases from J to J' because, for example, labour productivity increases, then (for a given U–V curve) we can conclude that equilibrium unemployment will be lower (U_1 to U_2) and vacancies higher (V_1 to V_2). Employment will increase ($L–U_1$ to $L–U_2$) but by a smaller amount than the increase in the number of jobs (J'–J). It is this last point that is important. Whilst an increase in the number of jobs in the economy increases employment and thus reduces unemployment, the effect is moderated in a dynamic labour market by the existence of vacancies. In other words some of the new jobs end up unfilled.

Finally we must consider the determination of and role played by wages. The problem in a dynamic labour market is that the concepts of supply and demand that are conventionally thought of as crucial in the determination of wages are no longer clear. Nevertheless there are good reasons for supposing that wages will respond to unemployment and vacancies. Whether wages are set by firms (see Chalkley (1988)), jointly by firms and individual workers (see Pissarides (1985a) or jointly by firms and unions (see Pissarides (1985b)), it is to

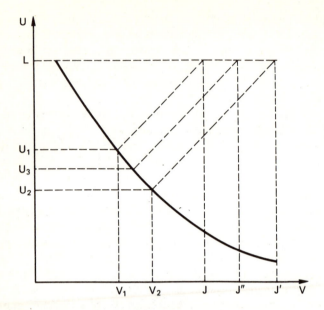

Figure 6.3   Determining equilibrium of the labour market.

be expected that wages will reflect the value of labour services and the scarcity of labour relative to jobs. I shall therefore regard the average level of wages as being positively related to some index of labour productivity, prices and the number of vacancies, and negatively related to the level of unemployment. The point U_2, V_2 in Figure 6.3 does not therefore tell the full story. If labour productivity were to rise, *other things being equal* the number of jobs will increase. However, we should also expect wages to rise for two reasons. First the increase in productivity will lead directly to higher wage demands. Second the increase in the stock of jobs will make vacancies harder to fill which will itself generate upward pressure on wages. Increased wages will therefore reduce the stock of jobs to something like J'' in Figure 6.3, with the consequence that in equilibrium unemployment falls only as far as U_3 not U_2. The final reduction in unemployment therefore depends upon the extent to which wages increase.

The simple model of a dynamic labour market that I have now outlined is in fact very powerful in analysing both the effects of conventional macro-economic and micro-economic policies aimed at reducing unemployment. Consider for example an attempt by the

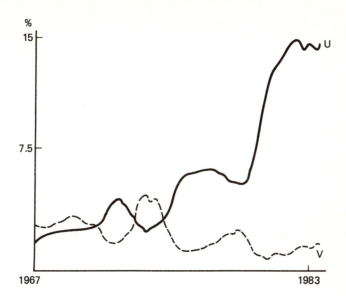

Figure 6.4   Vacancies and unemployment (% of working population).

government to stimulate aggregate demand in the economy. This might be reflected in higher prices for output or more simply an increase in the perceived productivity of labour if, for example, firms felt prior to the increase that they could not sell any more output. In any case Figure 6.3 is appropriate. The policy leads to job creation in the economy (the move from J to J'). This in turn stimulates wages and the final reduction in unemployment that is achieved depends upon the responsiveness of wages and the slope of the U–V curve.

What then of 'problem' unemployment in the UK? Over the last decade rising unemployment has been observed; vacancies on the other hand have remained more nearly constant (U and V are plotted in Figure 6.4). The data depicted in Figure 6.4 seem most easily explained by a shifting out of the U–V curve, perhaps because of increased mismatching or for the 'supply side' reasons indicated above.

Attempts at reducing 'problem' unemployment have largely been unsuccessful. It would seem that the kind of wage adjustment discussed above has proved very unfavourable to policies aimed at reducing unemployment. Stimulation of demand seems to have most of its impact upon prices and wages and really rather little effect upon unemployment. In terms of Figure 6.3 U_3 is in fact very close to U_1 after allowing for wage adjustment.

This has lead in turn to a consideration of 'supply-side' policies. There are a number of government-determined variables that might influence the decisions people make in respect of job acceptance or job search intensity. The generosity of unemployment benefits is thought, for example, to lead to more job rejection by the unemployed. Income taxes might similarly effect the incentives of individuals to seek out employment. Can supply-side policies like the reduction of tax rates and the restriction of unemployment benefits reverse the seeming drift to the right of the U–V curve and hence bring down unemployment? The evidence to date is not encouraging. Studies of the behaviour of unemployed individuals such as those of Nickell (1979) and Narendranathan *et al.* (1985) suggest that unemployment benefits in particular are not an effective tool in reducing unemployment. The evidence on taxes is somewhat less clear. The problem here, however, is that lower taxes may encourage participation so that L increases. At least as far as unemployment is concerned this moves things in the wrong direction. (It is quite simple to construct the appropriate U–V diagram to consider this case.)

The failure of conventional measures means that alternative policies such as the 1992 reforms come under the spotlight as potential cures. Can 1992 offer a solution to 'problem' unemployment according to this model? It is relatively straightforward to analyse the structural and aggregate (indirect) effects of 1992. I'll start with the aggregate effect.

6.2.2   Aggregate and structural effects

There are two sources of the aggregate effect. First, artificial barriers being removed will, it is claimed, lead to the exploitation of economies of scale and hence greater productivity. Second, greater competition in product markets will lead to lower prices. How then do these benefits feed into the labour market? A productivity increase is precisely what I considered in drawing Figure 6.3. There I argued that there would be an expansion in the number of jobs, perhaps tempered by increased wage demands. The new twist is that this may come about together with lower prices. At first sight this may appear to undo some of the good of increased labour productivity. There are, however, two reasons for supposing that this will not be the case and that jobs may be increased still further. First, if lower prices occur generally then firms will face lower input costs and this would imply an increase in J as firms expand output. Second, lower prices should reduce the pressure upon wages.

The structural effect arises because the relocation of production will cause an increase in the degree of mismatch in the labour market. This will result in a shift to the right of the U–V curve. It is possible that this shift would be so great as to lead to unemployment actually increasing even though the aggregate effect works to reduce unemployment. This, however, would appear to require a very large effect on the degree of mismatch. In any case the structural effect will serve to reduce the impact of the aggregate effect upon unemployment.

We should therefore expect a reduction in unemployment and an increase in vacancies and employment in accordance with Figure 6.3, offset by the structural effect and resulting shift in U–V as in Figure 6.2. How large will these effects be? The answer to this depends upon many things. The steeper is the U–V curve, for example, the more any increase in jobs will reduce unemployment. The increase in J depends in turn upon how firms and wages respond to higher productivity and lower prices. We cannot tell these things simply by looking at diagrams – we need instead an empirical model of the U.K. labour market. Such a model has been estimated by Pissarides (1986). I have estimated a similar model that more closely corresponds to the analysis of this section and used it first to derive estimates of the aggregate and structural effects as outlined above. The details of the method used are in the appendix to this chapter. The results are presented below:

Estimated changes in unemployment (U) and jobs (J) (000s) given:
(a) 1% reduction in prices and wages;
(b) 5% reduction in prices and wages;
(c) 5% reduction in prices and 2.5% reduction in wages.

Change in	Due to input prices	Due to output prices	Due to wages	Due to U	Total
a) U	– 68.9	143.0	–122.0		–47.9
J	125.0	–261.0	231.0	–37.0	58.0
b) U	–342.0	715.0	–610.0		–237.0
c) U	–342.0	715.0	–305.0		68.0

In viewing the numbers above it is important to remember that they are estimates. The imprecision with which any simple economic model can fit our observations of the labour market means that these estimates have a considerable degree of uncertainty attached to them.

The top two rows given above work through the estimated aggregate effect on the assumption that 1992 will reduce input and output prices and wages by 1 per cent. This is probably not an unreasonable starting point. Since 1992 will not affect all industries an overall effect of 1 per cent is quite significant. The implied reduction in UK unemployment is 47,900, or enough to have reduced the unemployment rate in 1987 from 9.75 per cent to 9.61 per cent of the workforce. If 1992 results in a 5 per cent reduction in prices and wages the reduction in unemployment is more significant and estimated to be 237,000. The assumption, however, that a reduction in prices feeds through fully into wages is a strong one and highly unrealistic. Most estimates of wage equations for the UK economy suggest that wages respond only slightly to downward price changes. Assuming that only half of the price reduction is passed on to wages results in an estimated reduction of unemployment of only 68,000, indicating that the adjustment of wages is crucial to any significant benefit flowing from the 1992 reforms. To show how the dynamic operation of the UK labour market is reflected in these estimates the estimated change in the stock of jobs is also reported. In the case of the 1 per cent price and wage effect, for example, the increase in the stock of jobs is 58,000. Along with fewer unemployed workers therefore there will be more unfilled jobs so that the reduction in unemployment is genuinely beneficial.

The structural effect further reduces any likely benefit but does not in fact eliminate it. If 1992 were to increase the degree of mismatching by 1 per cent my estimates suggest that unemployment would increase by 7,000. The net of aggregate and structural effects would therefore be a reduction of 40,900 in unemployment. The figures reported above can be modified quite easily to account for structural effects of varying magnitudes. The consequence will always be a lessening of the overall impact of 1992.

To conclude it is worth noticing two things. First, the above estimates suggest that 1992 will have a beneficial impact upon the UK labour market: unemployment will be reduced and the number of vacancies increased. This in turn implies shorter waiting times in the unemployment queue – 'problem' unemployment will be reduced. Secondly, however, unless 1992 has an implausibly large effect on prices, and, more particularly, wages within the UK any overall labour market effects are likely to be small.

6.3 1992 AND THE UK LABOUR MARKET: THE COMPOSITIONAL AND DIRECT EFFECTS

6.3.1 Regional considerations

In the previous section I analysed the likely overall impact of 1992 on UK unemployment. Whilst a quantification of the overall impact of 1992 is clearly important it is neither the only nor the most interesting question to address. One of the most documented facts about the UK labour market is the extent to which it generates regional disparities, particularly with respect to unemployment rates. The regional break-down of unemployment rates was reported in section 6.1. In this section I will consider how the model developed previously can be used to explain the regional disparities in unemployment and vacancies as a consequence of differing benefits to production in different regions. I will then consider the likely effect of the 1992 changes upon regional unemployment rates.

Consider again the model developed in the last section as an explanation of unemployment and vacancies in the UK. Suppose, however, that there are two labour markets – let us refer to them as North and South – and consider the interdependencies between the two. Two sorts of mobility are conceivable. Firms could choose to locate jobs in the most advantageous market or individuals could choose to pursue employment accordingly. The evidence for the UK indicates that neither firms nor individuals are particularly mobile across regions. I shall start by considering firms to be mobile and individuals fixed in their regions. To keep the arguments as simple as possible I shall also assume that initially both regions have the same number of individuals in their labour forces which I shall denote L^S and L^N respectively, the same number of jobs (J^S and J^N) and the same U–V curve. Wages need not be equal across the two regions but to the extent that there are wage differences these should reflect differences in either productivities or other production costs such that firms do not wish to move from one region to the other.

Now suppose that some change occurs such that production be-comes more favourable in the South. It is possible to show that an

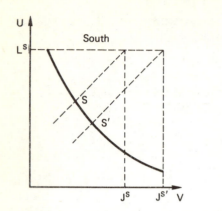
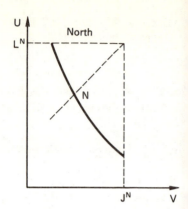

Figure 6.5   Equilibrium between workers and jobs.

equilibrium will emerge in which the South has lower unemployment than the North with more vacancies per unemployed worker. Furthermore this equilibrium will not necessarily be changed if workers are imperfectly mobile. I refer now to Figure 6.5.

Prior to the change there exist the same number of unemployed workers and vacant jobs in each region. With jobs made more profitable in the South we might expect an increase in job to $J^{S'}$. What sort of change might affect only one region in this way? It may be that production generally requires the use of an imported input and that the South is nearer the source of supply so that production costs are lower. Alternatively it may be that there is a change in the geographic location of the final market such that the South is simply nearer the market for goods and faces lower transport costs.

In any case there now exists a disparity between the two regions North and South. I claim it is possible that the points N, S' on the respective North and South U–V curves represent an equilibrium for each of the regional labour markets.

Compared with the initial equilibrium in which the regions were identical the South now has lower unemployment, more vacancies and more jobs than the North. It is the fact that firms in the South will now find it harder to attract employees to fill vacant jobs that will make jobs in the South less profitable than they otherwise would be. Notice also that the ratio of vacancies to unemployment is higher in the South and that this accords well with the data reported in section 6.1.

The operation of the labour market therefore serves to equalise the advantages of production as between regions. A point to notice is that we have not required wage adjustments between the two regions in order to equalise the advantages of production. It would be quite reasonable to expect the combination of more valuable production and more scarce labour to lead to upward pressure on wages in the South *relative* to the North. Wages, however, are often set by bilateral negotiation between employers and unions. Unions traditionally resist attempts to establish regional wage premia, perhaps because it is feared that employers may relocate employment to take advantage of lower wages. The evidence for the UK is that where regional wage differences for similar jobs exist they are in fact rather small. It seems reasonable therefore to assume that wages remain fixed across regions. Any general shift in wages that is precipitated by the change that I have considered above may alter the scale but not the regional disparities in unemployment and jobs that I have described.

The fact that the regions do not necessarily start as equals does not affect my conclusions either. A change that makes production in one region more favourable than another will tend to lower unemployment in the favoured region and raise it in the unfavoured region.

Will worker mobility serve to eliminate unemployment differentials? Whilst firms may be happy with the situation as depicted in Figure 6.5 – at least to the extent that no firm wishes to change the region in which it produces – there is a regional disparity as far as workers are concerned. By our assumptions the unemployed in the South face shorter queues for jobs but those jobs pay similar wages. We should therefore expect some migration of unemployed workers from North to South. At first glance it might appear that this migration would serve to equalise regional unemployment rates. I illustrate this point in Figure 6.6.

In Figure 6.6 the starting point is the equilibrium previously depicted in Figure 6.5. However, we are now supposing that unemployed workers relocate to the South. This has the effect of changing the regional workforces to $L^{S'}$ and $L^{N'}$ respectively. This in turn suggests equilibria at S'' and N' in the regional markets. It is possible that the movement in workers is sufficient to equalise unemployment rates in the two regions but this is rather unlikely. If it costs an unemployed worker to relocate (and the immobility of workers in practice suggests that such costs are high) then very large unemployment differentials will be required to induce only a few unemployed workers to relocate. It is important to realise that relocation costs include the costs to the individual of leaving family and friends as well

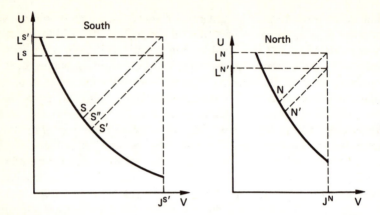

Figure 6.6   Effect of relocation of workers to the South.

as the monetary costs of moving. At best it is likely that mobility of individuals will mitigate slightly the impact of the change in the advantages of regional production upon unemployment disparities.

There is another reason for supposing that the migration of workers may not in fact serve to equalise unemployment across regions. Whilst wages may be as high and unemployment lower in the South other non-pecuniary advantages may be less. Road congestion, pollution and environmental factors may all lead to many unemployed workers feeling that the South is inferior to the North.

The kind of factors that led to the South becoming a low unemployment region in the above analysis may well be added to as 1992 approaches. The nearer proximity of the South to the European market both for output and for inputs suggest that firms may well wish to locate further South, particularly on completion of the Channel Tunnel. The above analysis suggests that as 1992 approaches disparities in regional unemployment rates may well widen. With costly mobility on the part of individuals there appears to be no mechanism by which any increase in regional disparities will be eliminated. These disparities are already a cause for concern in the UK context. What then of the possible policy responses to redress the balance? These may be of essentially two kinds: attempts to encourage firms back to the North, or incentives to encourage unemployed workers to the South.

Both selective employment subsidies and investment grants have long been considered both as an instrument for reducing total unemployment and as an aid to reversing the decline of regions within the national economy. Both of these measures are aimed at making the creation of jobs more worthwhile. It is not the purpose of this chapter to attempt a detailed critique of such policies. It is, however, worth raising one point. Many EC countries suffer from regional disparities of the kind I have considered. If these generally worsen as 1992 approaches we should expect a stepping up of regional policies throughout the Community. There are potential benefits from the coordination of such policies, or rather there are problems if coordination does not take place. One danger is that member countries essentially compete with each other through offering subsidies to their disadvantaged regions. It has long been realised that such actions might go against the spirit of the Treaty of Rome. The European Commission as long ago as 1965 published guidelines to the conduct of such policy. In recent years, however, regional policies have been in decline throughout Europe. In the UK for example regional aid has declined from £791 million in 1981–82 to £277 million in 1987–88. As a result of this general trend there has been very little recent concern about the coordination of such regional policies. The above analysis suggests that the incentives for regional policies particularly aimed at reducing unemployment differentials may well be increased as 1992 approaches. European countries will find the advantages of production moving towards the completed European market. This fact appears to have been overlooked in the Commission's own writings about the 1992 programme.

As for the mobility of workers, much of the recent concern in the UK has been with respect to distortions in the housing market and the implications these have for mobility costs (see Hughes and McCormick (1987)). The problem with moving people rather than jobs is that the prosperous regions of the UK are already the most densely populated. Congestion manifests itself in overcrowded roads and increasing development of 'greenfield' sites. Nevertheless there would appear to be some scope for alleviating regional unemployment disparities using, for example, changes in housing policies (see Hughes and McCormick (1981), McCormick (1983)). Our analysis suggests that such policies may become more urgent as 1992 approaches.

6.3.2 Skill composition

A second way of studying the compositional impact of 1992 is by distinguishing job and worker types. It is well known that disparities exist in unemployment rates between skilled and unskilled workers. In 1987, for example, the overall unemployment rate was 9.75 per cent. Skilled manual workers, however, faced 8 per cent unemployment whilst for semi-skilled workers the rate was 27 per cent.

More generally, between any particular category of jobs we might expect to observe differences in unemployment rates amongst individuals with skills oriented towards those jobs. One expected consequence of 1992 is presumably that the skill composition as well as the regional location of jobs will change. Indeed such a revision of skill composition of jobs underpinned our discussion of mismatch. The analogy between regional and skill compositions of the labour market is a strong one. Jobs can move from one skill type to another through investment in modern equipment whilst workers can move by retraining. There is therefore not a great deal of difference in formally modelling the impact upon skill composition to that which we conducted in relation to regional composition. In Figure 6.5, for example, we could label the left-hand diagram the labour market for 'skill S' and the right-hand that for 'skill N'. The differences that do exist between regions and skill types are more of degree rather than of fundamentals. Relative to the regional analogy we might expect jobs to be more mobile and workers less mobile, at least in the short run. Economists think of the skills of a worker as representing 'Human' capital. Like all capital, human capital requires investment and, in the case of skills, this investment takes time as well as expenditure.

Much of the above analysis therefore continues to hold. We might expect disparities with respect to the unemployment rates of different types of worker to widen with the approach of 1992. The policy response to this must, however, be different. Since it is workers who are now definitely less able to 'move' across skill types, policy must be aimed at retraining. Such policies of course already exist in the form of training and retraining programmes. The approach of 1992 may, however, make them more urgent.

6.3.3 Combining national labour markets

The direct impact of 1992 is reflected in specific labour market proposals involving the removal of barriers to labour mobility. These proposals account for only a single page in the 55-page White Paper from the Commission to the European Council. It is noted, for example, that the free mobility of employees is almost already legally ensured. The remaining problems are identified as being the tax treatment of workers who choose to live in one member country but work in another, rights of establishment for the self-employed and more general recognition across national frontiers of vocational and professional qualifications. There are no precise policy recommendations regarding these problems and subsequent reports make no mention of implementation. This is hardly surprising. Labour is not particularly mobile even within a single country. Social, economic and cultural factors that impede mobility are likely to be far more important across national frontiers and are not likely to be reduced significantly by legal reform. The direct effects of 1992 on labour markets therefore look like being of insignificant magnitude.

Within specific skill categories – most particularly those associated with the professions, however – the movement towards more European and less national markets for labour services may have some impact. This can be understood once again within the dynamic labour market model that I have considered. The consequence of combining national labour markets is to increase scale. If we take two entirely independent but identical national markets and combine them we achieve a single market of twice the size. Will this operate simply as a bigger version of the national markets? Often increases in scale are associated with resource savings. Indeed this is one of the supposed benefits of completing European product markets. A similar effect might arise from the combination of labour markets. In this case it may be reflected in the more efficient matching of workers to jobs. Doubling the number of vacancies and unemployed workers might lead to increased matching. The particular skills of an individual may suit only a very small number of jobs. Increasing the pool of both individuals and jobs will increase the chances of finding the right job for the right individual. There might therefore be an unexpected direct benefit of completing labour markets. Whether such a scale effect exists within the matching process that underlies the dynamic analysis of labour markets is a question that can only be addressed using empirical estimates of the matching relationship. This kind of work is very definitely in its infancy. The evidence such as it is, however, is not supportive of the idea. Pissarides (1986), for example, rejects the hypothesis of significant returns to scale in job–worker matching. The problem here is that Pissarides' analysis is for the labour market as a whole rather than for specialised skill types. It is still difficult, however, to imagine that the completion of professional labour markets will be at all wide ranging. Even within the professions cultural rather than economic variation across Europe will

considerably inhibit transnational migration. I do not therefore think
that the direct effects of 1992 are likely to be of significance.

6.4   CONCLUSIONS

The purpose of this chapter has been to assess the likely impact of the
1992 programme on the UK labour market. Apart from some basic
estimates of employment effects this is a neglected aspect in the
existing literature on 1992.

If we are first and foremost concerned with the possible beneficial
impact of 1992 upon the UK's unemployment problem it is crucial to
have an economic model consistent with observed facts about unemployment. To this end I have outlined a simplified framework within
which the UK labour market can be viewed. This framework sup-
poses that the UK labour market is in dynamic equilibrium, where
vacancies and unemployed workers coexist. It suggests that the
amount of unemployment observed is the consequence of the matching of unemployed workers to vacant jobs and depends also upon the
total number and type of jobs in existence in the economy. Each of
these may potentially be affected by the approach of 1992. In assessing the likely impact I identified some positive and some negative
components. The conclusion is therfore that the link between expanded output and increased employment is not as simple as the
existing literature on 1992 suggests. In order to produce some numerical estimates I estimated a model (as detailed in the appendix)
and concluded that the impact of 1992 on UK unemployment is likely
to be beneficial but small.

In section 6.3 I went on to consider some completely neglected
aspects of the approach of 1992 upon the regional and structural
composition of the UK labour market. In particular I have argued
that the relative immobility of labour suggests that it is likely that
regional disparities will widen and that in addition the skill composition of unemployment may alter, possibly requiring government
intervention, this particularly being the case if shortages of specialised labour are not to lead to the benefits of 1992 being dissipated. As
far as regional issues are concerned the analysis suggests that coordination between EC members may be necessary if wasteful regional
subsidies are not to result. On the direct effects of combining labour
markets across national frontiers there is little that can be said. On
any account, relative to the indirect effects that I have considered,

these direct consequences must be of secondary importance. The types of labour involved account for only a very small part of UK employment.

That labour market effects of 1992 are of interest is beyond doubt. That such effects have not been quantified and are in any case rather little understood is, I think, a cause for concern.

APPENDIX 6.1

In order to produce some numerical estimates of the impact via aggregate and structural effects of 1992 the following simple model of the UK labour market was estimated using quarterly data (1974 Q1 to 1988 Q1):

$$U = a_1 + b_1 U(-1) + c_1(U-4) + d_1 M + e_1 V$$

$$J = a_z + b_z J(-1) + c_z J(-4) + d_z W + e_z U + f_z P + g_z INPP$$

where:

U   = unemployment
V   = vacancies
J   = jobs (defined as the sum of vacancies and employment)
M   = mismatch measured by the year-on-year change in employment in
             construction and manufacturing industries
W   = a unit wage cost index
P   = producer price index
INPP = index of input prices
$U(-1)$= unemployment one quarter previously
$U(-4)$= unemployment four quarters previously.

Using the definition of J the above equations simultaneously determine U and V. These equations can be readily understood in the context of the model outlined in section 6.2. The equations were estimated using instrumental variables with the DFIT econometrics package. The resulting parameter estimates were then used to conduct simulations of the effect of 1992 as reported in section 6.2 above. The parameter estimates were as follows:

a_1	967.0	a_z	4,628
b_1	0.4097	b_z	0.3600
c_1	0.4721	c_z	0.5100
d_1	0.4730	d_z	−25.9
e_1	−3.70	e_z	0.1030
		f_z	30.6
		g_z	−16.7

I considered the long-run solution values and then considered changes in the mismatch, input price, labour cost and output price variables. The long-run solution for equilibrium unemployment implied by the estimates after solving for the simultaneous determination of U and V is:

$$U = 109.2W + 70.4INPP - 129.03P + 0.06997M$$

I used the values of these variables in 1988 quarter 1 to produce estimates of the impact of various percentage changes on unemployment. If further simulations are required the appropriate values to use are: W = 112.2, M = 10.0, P=111.0 INPP = 98.0. A solution for the total stock of jobs can then also be produced using the first equation.

References

Chalkley, M.J. (1991) 'Monopsony Wage Determination and Multiple Un-employment Equilibria in a Non-Linear Search Model', forthcoming in the *Review of Economic Studies*.

Hughes G. and McCormick, B. (1981) 'Do Council Housing Policies Reduce Migration Between Regions?', *Economic Journal*, 91, pp. 919–37.

Hughes G. and McCormick, B. (1987) 'Housing Markets, Unemployment and Labour Market Flexibility in the UK', *European Economic Review*, 9, pp. 615–45.

Junankar, P.N. and Price, S. (1984) 'An Anatomy of Unemployment Flows in Great Britain', Institute of Employment Research, University of War-wick, Discussion Paper No. 26.

McCormick B. (1983) 'Housing and Unemployment in Great Britain', Ox-ford Economic Papers, 35, pp. 283–305.

Narendranathan, N., Nickell, S.J. and Stern N. (1985) 'Unemployment Benefits Revisited', *Economic Journal*, 95, pp. 307–29.

Nickell, S.J. (1979) 'Unemployment and the Structure of Labour Costs', *Journal of Monetary Economics*, p. 11.

Nickell, S.J. (1982) 'The Determinants of Equilibrium Unemployment in Britain', *Economic Journal*, 92, pp. 555–75.

Pissarides, C.A. (1985a) 'Short-Run Equilibrium Dynamics of Unemploy-ment Vacancies and Real Wages', *American Economic Review*, 75, pp. 676–90.

Pissarides, C.A. (1985b) 'Dynamics of Unemployment, Vacancies and Real Wages with Trade Unions', *Scandinavian Journal of Economics*, 87, pp. 386–403.

Pissarides, C.A. (1986) 'Unemployment and Vacancies in Britain', *Econ-omic Policy*, 3, pp. 500–59.

7 Towards a European Financial Area

Philip Hardwick

7.1 INTRODUCTION

The financial services sectors of the member countries of the European Community have been growing in importance in recent years and now make substantial contributions to output and employment in all twelve countries. As shown in Table 7.1, financial services output in 1985 (measured by gross value-added) accounted for over 6 per cent of gross domestic product in the Community (the figure was almost 12 per cent for the United Kingdom) and employment in financial services industries accounted for about 3 per cent of total employment. Any gains which may result from integrating the financial sectors of the European Community by 1992 are likely, therefore, to have a significant effect on the economies of the member states, not least because all other sectors make use of financial services.

It is true to say that, by 1986, little progress had been made in harmonising the national rules and regulations governing financial activities and several countries still applied exchange controls on capital transactions. Yet it was in this year that the Single European Act came into force, stating that by 31 December 1992, all restrictions on capital movements must be lifted (without undermining exchange rate stability) and all discrimination affecting the free movement of financial services within the European Community must be abolished (without damaging the protection afforded to savers, fair competition or the stability of financial systems). The main benefits claimed for this liberalisation are lower costs of financial services and greater efficiency of financial markets resulting from the increase in competition. Nevertheless, there are some obstacles to liberalisation which will not be easy to remove and complete liberalisation is not without its drawbacks.

In section 7.2 of this chapter, we describe the present regulatory and administrative barriers which will have to be removed if a completely integrated financial area is to be achieved; also, we

Table 7.1   The relative sizes of European financial services sectors[1]

	Output as % of GDP	Employment as % of total employment
Belgium	5.7	3.8
France	4.3	2.8
Italy	4.9	1.8
Luxembourg	14.9	5.7
Netherlands	5.2	3.7
Spain	6.4	2.8
United Kingdom	11.8	3.7
West Germany	5.4	3.0
All 8 countries	6.4	2.9

[1] Defined to include all credit and insurance institutions.
[2] Measured by gross value-added.

Source: European Commission (1988), Table 5.1.1.

outline the European Community's proposals for the removal of the barriers. In section 7.3, the claimed benefits of an integrated market are considered critically, and in section 7.4, some of the possible drawbacks are discussed. The chapter ends with a brief conclusion in section 7.5.

7.2   THE PRESENT BARRIERS AND PROPOSED REFORMS

One of the principal barriers to financial integration in the European Community is the continued existence of exchange controls in some of the member countries. Although (at the time of writing) free capital movements are possible in the United Kingdom, West Germany and the Netherlands, there are still some controls in Belgium and Luxembourg (where reporting and authorisation procedures are required on some transactions in order to maintain a dual exchange rate system), and there are extensive controls in France, Spain, Greece, Portugal and Ireland. The European Commission proposes to have all exchange controls removed by the end of 1992, with a possible extension until 1995 for Greece and Portugal. The first stage of this was achieved in February 1987 when all cross-border transactions in unlisted securities, unit trusts, national securities issued on foreign stock exchanges and longer-term trade credits were liberalised. Foreign securities quoted on a stock exchange were also admitted to domestic markets. The second stage, which is intended to liberalise all further capital movements, is contained in a directive adopted in June 1988: this will apply to most of the member countries from July 1990 and to Spain, Greece, Portugal and Ireland from the end of 1992.

Complete freedom of capital movements, as well as being a prerequisite for the liberalisation of financial services in general, has possible implications for the independence of member countries' economic policies and the stability of the European Monetary System. These implications are discussed further in section 7.4. First, we turn to a consideration of other barriers to liberalisation and the specific proposals relating to the banking, insurance and securities sectors.

7.2.1 Banking

In addition to the continued application of exchange controls in certain countries, there remain a number of obstacles which act as barriers to the liberalisation of banking services. There is already a reasonable degree of *freedom to establish* for European Community banks in any member country in the sense that there are no regulatory barriers to establishment. This means that a bank may apply to a host country to open a branch office or a subsidiary and expect to be treated in the same way as domestic banks. Nevertheless, establishment costs vary substantially from country to country and in the high-cost countries it may be difficult for foreign banks to compete successfully with the existing local banks. Also, any bank seeking to establish in other countries has to seek authorisation in each country and, once established, will be subject to the diverse regulations and supervision of the host countries. In some member states, e.g. Italy and Spain, there are restrictions on foreign acquisitions and participations in local banks.

With respect to the sale of *cross-border* banking services, a number of discriminatory regulations are in force which restrict the services which banks are allowed to offer. Some rules actually prevent the soliciting of deposits across frontiers and in some countries there are limitations which prevent banks from engaging in securities business.

In its attempt to liberalise banking services, the European Commission has decided *not* to aim at harmonising all national regulations, but instead to aim at harmonising some of the basic rules and then operate the principles of *home country control* and *mutual recognition*. The cornerstone of the planned liberalisation of banking services is the Second Banking Co-ordination Directive, published in January 1988. According to this directive, there will be a single banking licence which will be issued to authorised banks together with an agreed list of banking activities. Once a bank has a licence, it will no longer need to obtain authorisation from the host country in order to open a branch office or establish a subsidiary in another European Community country, and it will be able to offer cross-border services without the present restrictions. For non-European Community banks to establish themselves in a member state on equal terms, they will have to satisfy various reciprocity arrangements, the details of which are currently contained in a draft directive. This is a worrying development for overseas (particularly United States) banks who are concerned with possible discrimination.

The concepts of home country control and mutual recognition mean that the primary task of supervision falls to the authorities in the bank's country of origin, with the host country having a minor complementary role. For this to work in practice, of course, each country must have trust in the regulations and the regulatory authorities in all other member countries. To this end, some harmonisation of rules is necessary and the Commission proposes to achieve commonality in the following matters:

(a) Own-fund requirements for European Community banks will be harmonised. These requirements will be separate from, but will conform with, the capital adequacy ratios proposed in by the Cooke Committee of the Bank for International Settlements (BIS). In July 1988, the BIS published an agreement reached by the Group of Ten (plus Luxembourg) on common standards for bank capital adequacy and for the measurement of bank capital. The main requirement is that the major commercial banks should hold capital equal to 8 per cent of their 'risk-adjusted assets' by the end of 1992, at least half of the 8 per cent being in the form of shareholders' equity (or 'core' capital). The BIS and European Commission proposals together will achieve a high degree of harmonisation with respect to required capital holdings by banks. It can be argued that they will make the financial system more efficient (by strengthening the stability of the international banking system) and more equitable (by removing the possibility of banks gaining a competitive edge by having a low capital base).

Nevertheless, McKenzie and Thomas (1991) have pointed out that a number of problems still remain to be resolved as different countries are likely to interpret the regulations in different ways.

(b) Banks and their major shareholders will have to disclose information concerning the size of their holdings and the identity of the owners. It is further proposed that banks' participation in non-financial companies should not exceed 10 per cent, with the total value of their holdings not normally exceeding 50 per cent of own funds.

(c) Banks' annual and consolidated accounts will be standardised to some extent so as to improve the comparability of accounts, though a number of accounting options will still be available to banks.

(d) Banks (and building societies) will be free to establish and to offer services in mortgage finance throughout the European Community under the supervision of the home country's regulatory authorities.

In addition, there are several other harmonisation proposals which affect taxation matters, cross-border mergers, takeovers and insider trading.

7.2.2 Insurance

In the insurance sector, there has been 'freedom of establishment' since the 1970s. As in banking, this means that there are no regulations preventing a foreign company from setting up a branch office or subsidiary. It does not mean, however, that it is a simple matter for an insurance company to establish itself in another member country. If a United Kingdom insurance company wished to open an office in France, for example, it would have to apply for a licence to operate as a French insurer and would then face double supervision by the British and French authorities: this could pose problems as regulations differ considerably from country to country. To ease the situation, some harmonisation of rules has been agreed (though very slowly) since the 1970s concerned with, for example, the minimum solvency margin that a company has to show and the procedures for granting authorisation.

There are, however, still many restrictions on the sale of cross-border insurance services. In fact, most member countries do not permit the insurance of risks in their country by insurers who are not authorised and established there. In 1986, proceedings were started in the European Court against France, West Germany, Denmark and Ireland for allegedly violating the Treaty of Rome in this regard. The judges ruled that it was not legitimate for governments to prevent the cross-border insurance of 'large risks' (by which is meant mainly industrial and commercial business for companies with a turnover of over ECU 24 million), though private individuals still required the protection of local supervision. This ruling would seem to open the door for cross-border 'large risk' insurance business where an individual consumer's protection is not at issue.

In cases where an individual consumer does need protection, a great deal more harmonisation of policy conditions and other rules is needed. The Commission aims to achieve freedom of services (by applying the 'home country control' and 'mutual recognition' principles) for small commercial business risks and personal life and non-life business, referred to as 'mass risks', by the end of 1992. Most commentators believe that it will take a good deal longer than that.

7.2.3 Securities

The main barriers to liberalisation in the stock market and securities sector (in addition, that is, to member countries' exchange controls) take the shape of a variety of national regulations. For example, there are prudential regulations which prevent foreigners from becoming brokers; there are in some countries discriminatory taxes on purchases of foreign securities; and there are certain restrictions on balance sheet holdings of foreign securities. Many of these barriers should be removed via directives before the end of 1992. A directive on investment services, would remove obstacles facing brokers, dealers and investment managers. Other directives will coordinate the protection of investors, allow simultaneous listings on member countries' stock exchanges and enable unit trusts to sell their units freely throughout the Community. Additionally, the stock exchanges in London, Paris, Milan, Madrid, Brussels, Amsterdam, Copenhagen, Dublin and Luxembourg are currently developing an 'Interbourse Data Information System' which should lead eventually to the creation of an electronic market for European securities.

Although by the end of 1992 there will undoubtedly remain some important obstacles to the complete liberalisation of financial services, significant strides will have been taken to allow both the freedom to establish and freedom of services for most financial services firms. This is regarded by many as an important step towards the creation of a European financial area.

7.3 THE POTENTIAL GAINS

The principal gains claimed for the liberalisation of financial markets in the European Community stem mainly from the expected reductions in the prices of financial products. As regulatory barriers are removed so that cross-border trade in financial services becomes easier, there should be a shift in demand away from higher-cost suppliers towards lower-cost suppliers. In the jargon of customs union theory, this is trade creation which should benefit consumers throughout the Community. As the consumers of financial services include nearly all individuals and businesses in all European countries, the potential gains from this source are substantial. Cecchini (1988) argues that lower capital costs will encourage aggregate investment and so increase the rates of economic growth of the member countries. He further suggests that the lower prices of financial services will 'radiate a deflationary surge through the economy at large' so that 'households will benefit doubly: they will pay less for financial services and will gain from the general drop in prices'. The European Commission itself estimates that the gains from this source will amount to approximately ECU 22 billion. These gains do depend, however, on (a) the complete removal of all regulatory barriers and (b) the absence of other obstacles to trade in financial services. It is not at all clear that either (a) or (b) can be achieved by the end of 1992.

The extent of the expected reductions in the prices of financial services in the member states is, of course, extremely difficult to estimate with confidence. In a study undertaken by Price Waterhouse (International Economic Consultants), and reported in *European Economy* (1988), the potential price reductions were analysed for a wide range of financial products in eight of the member countries. Financial products were categorised into banking, insurance and brokerage services: seven banking services, five insurance services and four brokerage services were identified and the cost (measured in ECUs) of a 'standard' service was estimated in each of the eight member states using sample information. The average of the four lowest prices for each service was taken to represent the 'competitive'

Table 7.2   Potential price reductions

| | Theoretical potential price reductions (%) | | | |
	Banking	Insurance	Brokerage	All financial services
Belgium	15	31	52	23
France	25	24	23	24
Italy	18	51	33	29
Luxembourg	16	37	9	17
Netherlands	10	1	18	9
Spain	34	32	44	34
United Kingdom	18	4	12	13
West Germany	33	10	11	25

Source: Price Waterhouse (1988), Table 5.1.4.

price which would prevail under conditions of complete liberalisation – this presumably is the price which would be expected in the long run under conditions of perfect competition with constant costs. The differences between the observed prices and the 'competitive' prices were calculated for each service in each country and these were interpreted as the *potential* falls in price resulting from liberalisation. The results of this exercise for banking, insurance and brokerage services are shown in Table 7.2, together with the average price reductions for all financial services in the eight member states.

Recognising that, even after the removal of all regulatory barriers, some obstacles and imperfect competition will persist, Price Waterhouse quite arbitrarily converted the potential price falls into *expected* price falls by reducing the potential falls by about one-half (with some variations for countries where circumstances suggested a higher or lower adjustment). An interval of plus-or-minus 5 per cent around the resulting figures was then calculated to allow for a margin of error. These results are shown in Table 7.3; the estimated gains in consumer surplus, measured both in ECUs and as a percentage of GDP, are also shown for the eight countries included in the study. The gains in consumer surplus were calculated on the assumption that the elasticity of demand for financial services is 0.75.

The results indicate that Spain is expected to benefit most in terms of price reductions, followed by Italy, France, Belgium and West Germany. The United Kingdom and the Netherlands face the lowest expected reductions. Although only relatively small price reductions are expected for the United Kingdom (between 2 and 12 per cent),

Table 7.3   Expected price falls and gains in consumer surplus

	Expected price falls (%)	Gains in consumer surplus ECU billions	% of GDP
Belgium	6–16	0.7	0.7
France	7–17	3.7	0.5
Italy	9–19	4.0	0.7
Luxembourg	3–13	0.1	1.2
Netherlands	0–9	0.3	0.2
Spain	16–26	3.2	1.5
United Kingdom	2–12	5.1	0.8
West Germany	5–15	4.6	0.6

Source: Price Waterhouse 1988, Table 5.1.5.

the expected gain in consumer surplus is seen in Table 7.3 to be quite substantial (ECU 5.1 billion or 0.8 per cent of GDP). This is explained by the relatively large size of the financial services sector in the United Kingdom. The other major beneficiaries in terms of the expected gains in consumer surplus are Luxembourg and Spain.

The results of the Price Waterhouse study seem very promising, but one has to be very sceptical of the calculated numerical estimates. For one thing, financial products are heterogeneous and this makes international cost comparisons very hazardous indeed. It is particularly difficult to define 'standard' insurance products in different countries where there are undoubtedly different levels of risk. For example, in countries where premiums on theft insurance are low, companies may well charge higher premiums for the same policies sold in countries where the risk of theft is greater. The same kind of argument can be applied to other financial products. Furthermore, the removal of regulatory barriers is not synonymous with the creation of a perfectly competitive market. Imperfect competition, the possible failure to remove all administrative barriers, the continued existence of imperfect information about which cross-border services are available and international differences in risks, customs, languages and other conditions will all contribute to a high margin of error in the estimates. The conclusion that all member countries should enjoy average price *reductions* seems particularly optimistic. Given the high margin of error, it is possible that the lower-cost countries (for example, the Netherlands and the United Kingdom), which should experience an increase in cross-border demand for many of their financial services following the removal of barriers, will face price rises in the short term, and possibly in the long term.

Also, it should be emphasised that, in countries which do experience price falls, some proportion of the increase in consumer surplus will be offset by a decrease in producer surplus. There is little doubt that the opening up of financial markets will squeeze profits throughout the sector and many financial institutions will face a bleak prospect as a result. There will be losers among those institutions which have relatively high costs and little international experience. The gainers will be those which can take advantage of the new opportunities.

7.3.1　Dynamic effects

The above discussion is concerned mainly with the static effects of liberalisation. Other potential gains are those associated with the dynamic production effects, i.e. those which result from economies of scale and the surge in competition.

With regard to economies of scale, the argument is that the present segmentation of the European financial services market means that European financial institutions have not been able to take full advantage of the available economies of scale. The opening up of the market should enable many of the more efficient firms to expand and so benefit from lower unit production costs. This argument is not entirely convincing. First, many European financial institutions are already very large and have considerable overseas business within and outside Europe: this is certainly true of many banks in the United Kingdom, West Germany, Spain and France and the larger insurance companies in the United Kingdom. Secondly, it is not at all certain that there are economies available. Studies of banking in the United States and building societies in the United Kingdom suggest that diseconomies of scale are more likely above a certain size. One has to be doubtful, therefore, whether there will be unit cost savings resulting from the further expansion of the larger European financial services firms. Growth and mergers among small and medium-sized institutions may yield economies of scale, but such firms will probably be taken over by the giants.

Will the surge in competition lead to greater efficiency, an increase in the rate of innovation and further price reductions? The removal of the regulatory restrictions on cross-border trade should increase the degree of competition in the early years. However, the longer-term effects of this are debatable: small operations may not be able to survive, there may be more takeovers and mergers with a consequent increase in concentration. As an example, the increase in competition in the United Kingdom building society industry in recent years has contributed to the rapid decline in the number of societies and there is every sign that this will continue with the opening up of cross-border trade in mortgage finance. If there is an increase in concentration, will the net result of liberalisation be an increase or decrease in competition? It is impossible to say, but the prospect of universal banks undertaking all kinds of financial services (like one-stop financial supermarkets) certainly suggests the possibility that the market will eventually be dominated by huge oligopolistic institutions, with few small or medium-sized firms surviving.

7.4 SOME WORDS OF CAUTION

Financial liberalisation, including the removal of all exchange controls, has implications for the stability of the European Monetary System (EMS). The following simplified scenarios describe four situations within which the EMS may be operated:

(a) Imperfect capital mobility with no economic policy coordination;
(b) Imperfect capital mobility with economic policy coordination;
(c) Perfect capital mobility with no economic policy coordination;
(d) Perfect capital mobility with economic policy coordination.

An acceptable degree of exchange rate stability (by which is meant the avoidance of frequent and excessive parity adjustments) should be possible under situations (a), (b) and (d). In situation (a), restrictions on capital movements enable countries to follow independent economic policies without seriously destabilising the exchange rates. Situation (b) is also dynamically stable, but is unlikely to occur because without capital mobility, the incentive to coordinate policies is reduced. In situation (d), coordinated policy actions (particularly, though not exclusively, in the field of monetary policy) are the means by which capital flows can be prevented from having a destabilising effect.

Unfortunately, it is (c) which probably best describes the situation towards which the European Community is moving. The removal of exchange controls by 1992 will lead to a high degree of capital mobility. Without improved coordination in policy-making by the member states, this mobility may increase the frequency and size of exchange rate adjustments, thus transforming the EMS from a relatively fixed exchange rate regime into a relatively flexible one. In the 1980s, the EMS has remained reasonably stable, partly because capital mobility has been imperfect and partly because of the achievement of basic agreements on policy objectives (principally the avoidance of inflation) by the member states. It seems clear, however, that the removal of exchange controls will necessitate the integration of policy instruments as well as a general agreement on policy objectives if the EMS is to be maintained as a relatively fixed exchange rate regime. Unfortunately, this will involve some loss of sovereignty which may not be acceptable to some member states.

The changes proposed for 1992 are seen by many as further steps along the path leading to the creation of a European financial area with a common currency and a common central bank. This is a misguided view, in my opinion. It is true that the removal of exchange controls, and the resulting improvement in capital mobility, helps to satisfy one of the preconditions for an *optimum* currency area, as defined by Mundell (1961). The problem is that the other precondition (mobility of labour) will not be achieved by 1992. Labour tends to be immobile intranationally for a variety of well-known reasons: international mobility is further hampered by language and cultural differences. This means that a common currency area (or, equivalently, a rigidly fixed exchange rate regime with common economic policies) within the European Community, as well as involving a loss of sovereignty, would probably be characterised by high 'regional' unemployment rates.

So how far should the European Community go towards the creation of a European financial area? Taking into account the diversity of the member states, perhaps the best that can be achieved is the compromise solution proposed for 1992: a compromise in which there is an exchange rate regime with some degree of flexibility, a high degree of free trade in financial services, free movement of capital (unless balance of payments or exchange rate difficulties arise) and improved coordination in the policy actions taken by the member states.

7.5 CONCLUSIONS

Three main conclusions may be drawn from this chapter. First, it is improbable that *all* regulatory and administrative barriers with respect to financial services will be removed by 1992, though substantial progress will undoubtedly have been made by that 'magic' date. In particular, some restrictions on cross-border insurance business will remain and the varying costs of establishment between one country and another will continue to restrict establishment in high-cost countries. Secondly, the advantages claimed for financial liberalisation have been exaggerated by many commentators: net gains to consumers should result from the removal of barriers, but the estimated price reductions are probably overstated, there is a possible loss of producer surplus and there is little evidence of substantial 'dynamic' gains. Thirdly, the attainment of the 1992 objectives should be seen as creating more open markets in the European Community and not as a step towards the eventual creation of a common currency area.

References

Benston, G.J., Handweck, G.A. and Humphries, D.B. (1982) 'Scale Economies in Banking: A Restructuring and Reassessment', *Journal of Money, Credit and Banking*, 14, pp. 435–56.

Cecchini, P. (1988) *The European Challenge: 1992*, Gower, London.

European Commission (March 1988) 'The Economics of 1992', *European Economy*, special issue, pp. 1–222.

Hardwick, P. 'Multi-product Cost Attributes: A Study of UK Building Societies', *Oxford Economic Papers*, 42, pp. 446–461.

McKenzie, G. and Thomas, S. (1991) *Financial Instability and the International Debt Problem*, Macmillan, London.

Mundell, R. (1961) 'A Theory of Optimum Currency Areas', *American Economic Review*, 51, 657–65.

8 Monetary Policy and the EMS

John Driffill and Paul Turner

8.1 INTRODUCTION

There exists no clear-cut argument either in favour of or against UK membership in the exchange mechanism of the EMS. The arguments that it will entail the UK in further losses of sovereignty and freedom of independent action in monetary policy are ranged against the view that membership will enhance the credibility of the government's anti-inflationary stance and allow the economy to enjoy the benefits of lower interest rates, closer to those of Germany. In 1989 the Chancellor of the Exchequer, Nigel Lawson, favoured entry while Prime Minister Margaret Thatcher's camp did not. Meanwhile, as the arguments in the UK go backwards and forwards, in Europe as a whole the movement towards integration proceeds. For monetary policy and exchange rates this means increasing the coordination of monetary policies, reducing the variation in exchange rates, and removing controls on transactions associated with capital movements. Further ahead is foreseen more complete monetary union with a single currency and a European central bank.

In April 1989 the report of the Delors committee was published, setting out broad proposals for further steps on the road to complete economic and monetary union in the Community. They proposed a three-stage process. The first stage involves changes to take place within the existing institutional structure, involving increased cooperation and coordination in monetary policy, and leading up to a change in the Treaty of Rome. Realignments would remain possible, but capital movements would be completely free, and financial, banking and insurance services offered uniformly and freely throughout the EC. All Community members would belong to the exchange rate mechanism of the EMS. The second stage would follow the coming into force of the new Treaty, and involve setting up 'basic organs and structure of the monetary union' (Delors Committee Report, 1989, p. 32). This would involve, *inter alia*, setting up a

European System of Central Banks (ESCB), with the task (at this stage) of making the transition from independent monetary policies to the formulation and implementation of a common European monetary policy. The margins of fluctuation of EMS currencies would be narrowed, with a target of zero margins. The final stage would involve the move to 'irrevocably locked exchange rates' (Delors Committee Report, 1989, p. 35), and the replacement of separate currencies by a single Community currency. 'The rules and procedures of the Community in the macro-economic and budgetary field would become binding.' These may involve placing constraints on national budgets to prevent imbalances that might threaten monetary stability. The committee did not give a timetable for these changes, which will presumably come (if at all) some years after 1992.

There is thus increasing pressure on the UK to participate fully in the EMS by joining the exchange rate mechanism, as part of the package of policies tied up with the Single European Act. Eventual participation by the UK appears to be inevitable, whatever the current official reservations. This prospect raises questions about how monetary and exchange rate policy in the UK will be affected. Indeed, fiscal policy may be affected by membership in a strengthened exchange rate mechanism, as restricted monetary freedom spills over into limits on sustainable budgetary policy. In order to look at these questions in more detail, we first review the structure and method of operation of the existing EMS and examine the ways in which it has affected economic policy and macroeconomic performance in Europe. We then turn to an examination of the proposed developments of the system, including the removal of capital controls and extended credit facilities available to members for intervention in foreign exchange markets. In the light of all this, we consider the arguments over membership and detail its likely implications for the UK. The longer-term prospects are for monetary union, a single European currency and a European central bank, as the Delors report sets out. The later parts of the paper analyse these possibilities. The concluding section of the paper summarises the main points in the story and offers our overall evaluation of the implications of the EMS and 1992 in the field of macroeconomic policy and performance in the UK.

8.2 EMS: STRUCTURE AND RECENT DEVELOPMENTS

8.2.1 The structure of the EMS

The EMS began operation on 13 March 1979. It was intended (a) as a successor to the various arrangements which were used during the 1970s, generally referred to as 'the Snake', (b) as a move in the direction of greater exchange rate stability within the EC, and (c) as a means of encouraging greater convergence of monetary policies within the Community. The Exchange Rate Mechanism (ERM) of the system prescribes that exchange rates between participants should be kept within narrow bands. There are provisions for realignments of these bands from time to time, and rules for intervention in foreign exchange markets to keep exchange rates within them. When the system was set up in 1979, Britain stayed out of the ERM, while the other then EEC member countries – Denmark, West Germany, the Netherlands, Belgium, Luxemberg, France, Italy and Ireland – joined.

The ERM prescribes a set of parity exchange rates between each pair of currencies (bilateral central rates), and around these are set limits within which exchange rates are allowed to vary. These limits are 2.25 per cent above and below the parity for all countries except Italy, for which they are 6.0 per cent. The lira/deutschmark rate, the franc/deutschmark rate and their bilateral limits are illustrated in Figures 8.1 and 8.2. When the exchange rate between any pair of currencies reaches an upper or lower limit of fluctuation, the central banks of the two countries involved are required to intervene in order to prevent the exchange rate from straying outside the band. The central bank whose currency is 'weak' is obliged to sell the 'strong' currency on demand, and the central bank with the 'strong' currency is obliged to buy the weak currency.

In practice countries are free to intervene in exchange markets before exchange rates reach the edges of the bands, if they want to. This kind of intra-marginal intervention has been used quite a lot, usually with the mutual agreement of the two central banks involved, to damp down movements of exchange rates inside the bands. In addition, intra-marginal intervention may be stimulated by the *divergence indicator*, which will be described below.

The set-up of the EMS has given importance to a currency unit called the ECU. The European Currency Unit (ECU) is a basket containing a prescribed amount of each EMS currency. For each

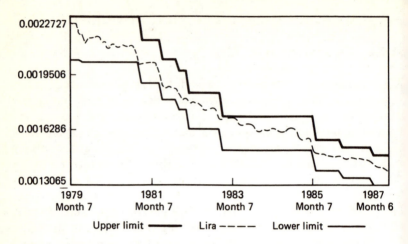

Figure 8.1   Lira/deutschmark exchange rate and limits of fluctuation
(no. of DM to 1 lira).

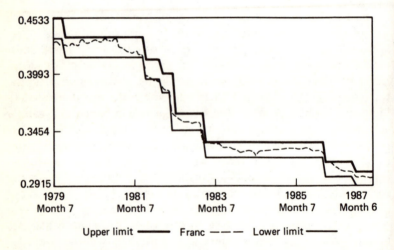

Figure 8.2   Franc/deutschmark exchange rate and limits of fluctuation
(no. of DM to 1 franc).

currency can be calculated (a) the price of 1 ECU when all currencies
are priced at the parity rate of exchange, and (b) the price of 1 ECU
when all currencies are priced at the actual market rate of exchange.
The first (a) gives the ECU-related central rate of the currency, and
the second (b) gives the actual market rate of exchange between the
currency and the ECU. The percentage difference between them is a

weighted average of the depreciation or appreciation of the currency against all others in the system, and is called the *divergence spread*. If a currency were to appreciate by 2.25 per cent relative to all others, the divergence spread would achieve the highest value it could take, and this value is denoted the maximum divergence spread. The divergence indicator is the ratio of the actual value of the divergence spread to the maximum divergence spread. When the divergence indicator reaches a value of 75 per cent, then a divergence threshold is said to have been reached, and at this point there is a presumption that the government of the country in question will take some action to stabilise the exchange rate. This can take a number of forms, which include:

(a) intervention in foreign exchange markets;
(b) domestic monetary policy actions, such as changing minimum lending rate (or its equivalent), open market operations, and other actions which affect interest rates;
(c) other domestic policy action, such as fiscal policy or incomes policy;
(d) changing the parity exchange rate, with the argreement of other EMS member countries.

If a country fails to act in the appropriate way when the divergence threshold is reached, then it is required to explain why to other EMS governments, and this provides a trigger for consultations among member governments about macroeconomic policy generally and exchange rates in particular.

8.2.2 Financing of exchange market intervention in the EMS

A country whose currency is at the bottom of the allowed band is required by the EMS to defend its value, unless the member countries jointly agree a realignment of parities, by intervening in the foreign exchange market. The system has a number of provisions for enabling it to do so. A country whose currency is depreciating – Italy, say – might be required under these rules to sell German marks (for example) in whatever quantities are needed to keep the mark/lira exchange rate within ± 6.0 per cent of parity. In order to ensure that the Italian central bank (the Banca d'Italia) is able to meet this obligation, there are provisions for the central banks to lend each other their currencies for shorter or longer periods.

Very short-term financing consists of loans provided by one central bank to another, in quantities which are in principle unlimited, for an initial period of 45 days, in order to enable intervention to keep currencies inside the bands. There are provisions also for short-term monetary support, and medium-term financial assistance. These are described in great detail in van Ypserele (1985). They provide limited amounts of foreign exchange to countries with balance of payments problems in the EMS, but over longer periods of time.

8.2.3 Realignments in the EMS and the use of capital controls

The above paragraphs describe the way in which the EMS tries to preserve an existing set of parity exchange rates. It contains also provisions for changing parity exchange rates from time to time by agreement among participants. There were realignments in the EMS on 24 September 1979, 30 November 1979, 22 March 1981, 5 October 1981, 22 February 1982, 14 June 1982, 21 March 1983, February 1986 and November 1986. Not all of these involved all the participating currencies. The lira, for example, was devalued relative to the mark on eight of these occasions. This experience suggests that there has been a fair degree of willingness to use the option of realignment of exchange rates under the EMS.

Many of these realignments would not have been possible without the capital controls which many ERM countries have maintained. France and Italy have had restrictions on the ability of residents of those countries to buy and sell financial assets in other currencies, and Belgium and Luxembourg maintain a system of two-tier exchange rates. Foreign exchange transactions which are related to trade go through the official market in which the National Bank of Belgium (NBB) intervenes. Those related to acquisitions and disposals of foreign assets by domestic residents and of domestic assets by foreign residents go through the financial exchange market, in which the NBB does not officially intervene, and in which the price of the Belgian franc typically stands at a discount relative to the price on the official market.

These capital controls have smoothed the process of realignment by preventing large speculative capital outflows against depreciating currencies. When a currency is expected to be devalued, there is a strong incentive for holders of the weak currency to sell assets denominated in it, and buy assets in the strong currency. In order to maintain the value of the weak currency before the devaluation actually occurs, the central bank is obliged to buy up its own currency and meet the demand for the strong currency. The cost of this to the central bank is roughly the difference between the cost of the foreign exchange at the (higher) post-devaluation price and its value at the (lower) pre-devaluation price. The central bank's loss is the speculators' gain. As an alternative to intervention in foreign exchange markets, the central bank might try to raise interest rates to discourage speculative capital outflows by making the lost interest greater. However, when markets expect a devaluation to occur within a short time, very large increases in short-term interest rates tend to be needed.

The ability of the EMS to survive so many realignments has been a source of surprise to many observers. It has been explained by a combination of capital controls, and by making the timing of devaluations hard to predict, so that speculators do not perceive a (more or less) certain gain to be made within a short period of time. This has meant revaluing fairly frequently, typically not letting the pressure for devaluation build up to the point where an immediate devaluation is almost certain, and allowing governments to retain some freedom over the timing and extent of realignment.

There is continuing movement towards the removal of capital controls, and free movement of capital throughout Europe by 1992 is an important aspect of the Single European Market. This objective raises a large question as to how the EMS will be able to survive in such a situation. It is, broadly speaking, clear that with unrestricted capital flows, realignments of exchange rates will have to be much smaller than in the past, and may have to be small enough to leave the current market exchange rate inside the realigned band, so that there would be no jump in the actual exchange rate. This requires that EMS countries keep their price levels closely in line with each other. Hence this requires continued movement towards the coordination of monetary and fiscal policy among EMS countries. The implications of removing capital market restrictions are discussed in more detail below.

8.2.4 Macroeconomic convergence under the EMS

At the time of the establishment of the EMS, its members had very different inflation rates, as Figure 8.3 illustrates. In July 1979, for example, the annual inflation rate in West Germany was 5 per cent, in France 10 per cent and in Italy 14 per cent. During 1980, the differences in inflation rates widened considerably, before they began

144 *John Drifill and Paul Turner*

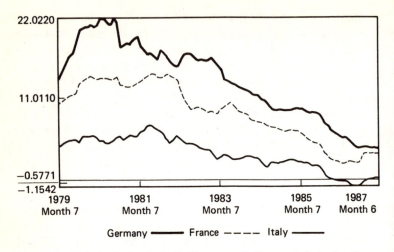

Figure 8.3   Inflation rates in Italy, France and Germany (calculated as the percentage increase in the consumer price index in each country over its value one year earlier).

to narrow from 1981 on. Under such circumstances, a set of fixed exchange rates would have been unsustainable: the competitiveness of Italy relative to West Germany would have fallen by 9 per cent a year at the July 1979 inflation rates. It was for that reason that the EMS was set up in such a way as to allow periodic changes in exchange rates.

While the purpose of the EMS was at least in part to accommodate the differences in inflation rates between member countries, it was intended that those differences should gradually disappear. The stated aim of the EC has been to achieve a common low inflation rate across the community, one which would be consistent with maintaining fixed exchange rates between the member countries and, ultimately, a single European currency. Figure 8.3 illustrates that some convergence of inflation rates has been achieved.

The role of the EMS in achieving low inflation is not entirely clear. Two arguments are offered. One is that the high inflation countries of the EC (such as Italy) wanted in any case to reduce their inflation rate, and would have taken policy action to achieve it regardless of the exchange rate regime. Italy's willingness to join the EMS was just a reflection of that. On this reading of events, the EMS has played no role in bringing about convergence of inflation rates: it would have happened anyway.

The opposing view is that the EMS has acted as a constraint on Italian macroeconomic policy, inducing Italian governments to adopt tighter monetary and fiscal policies than they otherwise would have done. It is argued that Italian governments, with their history of high inflation and unsuccessful attempts to stabilise prices, would have been unable to make announcements about plans to reduce inflation in such a way that these plans would have been believed by Italians. Workers would have continued to achieve rapid increases in money wages, and faced with these wage increases, the government would have been forced by domestic pressures to allow domestic prices to rise and the exchange rate to fall proportionately (broadly speaking) in order to maintain employment. By entering into an agreement with other countries, the Italian government is able to make its anti-inflationary plans more credible. The reason is that once inside the EMS, it becomes less attractive for the government to accommodate wage increases and inflation, either because a devaluation would become necessary (this is more difficult to negotiate inside the EMS than it is when the lira is simply floating) or because, in the absence of devaluation, the effect of higher wage rates is to reduce domestic output and employment. This 'credibility' aspect of the EMS has been analysed extensively by Giavazzi and Giovannini (1988).

Whether or not the EMS has played a role in bringing it about, there has been a clear convergence of inflation rates among countries in the ERM, and correspondingly a need for less frequent realignments in recent years.

8.2.5 Exchange rate volatility in the EMS

An argument made in favour of managed exchange rates is that they may eliminate some of the wilder fluctuations of exchange rates which have occurred when they are allowed to float freely. The US dollar and the pound have been highly volatile in the early 1980s, for example, as Figure 8.4 illustrates.

It is important here to distinguish between nominal and real exchange rates. The nominal rate is the price of £1 in terms of US dollars, for example. The real rate is the relative price of a given basket of goods in the two countries, expressed in a common currency. If E_t is the sterling price of \$1, P_t is the price level in the UK, and P_t^* is the price level in the USA, then the real exchange rate is $P_t^* E_t / P_t$ – the sterling price of a unit of goods bought in the US, relative to the sterling price of a unit of goods bought in the UK. The

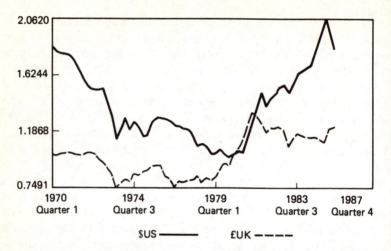

Figure 8.4   Real exchange rates: £UK/DM and $US/DM (calculated
              as the exchange rate multiplied by the ratio of consumer price
              indices for the pair of countries involved and normalised to
              take the value 1.0 in the first quarter of 1980).

real exchange rate is often called 'competitiveness' since it gives an
indication of the relative prices of domestically produced and imported goods which is the key variable which determines consumers'
choices between them.

   Volatility of nominal rates may be unimportant if the real exchange
rate moves merely so as to offset differences in national inflation
rates, leaving the real exchange rate constant. The problem of
floating exchange rates in the 1970s and 1980s has been that nominal
exchange rate movements have not moved so as to offset inflation
differences, and have contributed a large proportion of the fluctuations in real exchange rates which have occurred. There are several
reasons why nominal exchange rates might behave this way under a
regime of floating. These all depend on the fact that in the absence of
government intervention exchange rates depend largely on expectations of the future.

   Nominal exchange rates within the EMS are managed, and this has
contributed to less real exchange rate variation inside the EMS than
outside it. There has been some variation in real rates among West
Germany, France and Italy since 1979, as Figure 8.5 shows. Nor-
malising both real rates (Italy/Germany and France/Germany) to
1.00 in January, the Italian rate had risen to 1.21 in early 1985, while

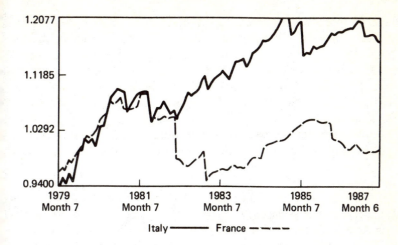

Figure 8.5 Real exchange rates of Italy and France relative to Germany (calculated as the exchange rate multiplied by the ratio of consumer price indices for the pair of countries involved and normalised to take the value 1.0 in the first quarter of 1980).

the French rate fluctuated between 0.95 and 1.08 in the period to June 1987. During periods between realignments, the competitiveness of both France and Italy relative to Germany fell, since they had faster inflation. At times of realignment, Italian competitiveness has been restored only partly back towards its former level. It is argued that allowing Italian goods to become less competitive relative to the rest of the ERM countries is one of the ways in which demand for goods in Italy has been restrained and the inflation rate decelerated. In France, competitiveness has been largely restored, and sometimes more than restored, at times of realignment. Since the beginning of 1982, the real exchange rate between France and Germany has been kept roughly within 5 per cent of its January 1980 value.

Thus, while real exchange rates may have varied considerably in the EMS, it may be argued that such variations which have occurred have been, at least in part, the result of conscious policy actions.

8.2.6 Interest rate volatility in the EMS

It has often been argued that while exchange rates may be less variable inside the EMS rather than outside it, interest rates will become more volatile, since, when a currency tends to depreciate, central banks have first to intervene in the foreign exchange market by buying up excess supplies of the currency, and, if and when this is inadequate to maintain the exchange rate within the permitted bounds, to take some further action, and this has typically taken the form of raising interest rates. When financial markets expect that a devaluation of a currency is likely to occur, people become unwilling to hold assets denominated in it unless the rate of return on them is high enough to offset the risk of devaluation. This tends to cause interest rates to rise dramatically when the conditions for such a realignment occur.

In the case of France and Italy, which have persistently devalued their currencies against the German mark, interest rates inside the countries have not fluctuated much because controls on capital movements have prevented people in those countries from buying foreign currencies. However, 'offshore' interest rates have fluctuated considerably (see Giavazzi and Giovannini (1988)). 'Offshore' rates are those paid on deposits held in, say, French francs by non-residents of France outside of France, and thus not subject to French capital market restrictions and controls, in the Eurocurrency markets. In 1986, for example, prior to the realignment of April, the domestic rate on 1-month deposits in France remained at around 9 per cent per annum, while the offshore rate reached 18 per cent. More dramatic differences appeared in 1982 and 1983 (again, see Giavazzi and Giovannini (1988)). Thus there has been some evidence of increased interest rate volatility inside the EMS, largely suppressed by use of capital controls.

There is, however, no reason why a system such as the EMS should necessarily entail greater interest rate volatility than a system of floating exchange rates. The amount of volatility depends largely on the monetary and fiscal policies pursued by the member countries, and to a smaller degree on the kinds of external shocks – such as changes in oil or primary commodity prices – which affect them. When the EMS was set up in 1979, the member countries were pursuing very different macroeconomic policies and had very different inflation rates, and frequent realignments were needed. Much of the interest volatility was associated with realignments. When members pursue policies consistent with roughly similar inflation rates, so that any realignments are smaller and/or less frequent, they are able to maintain more or less similar interest rates. In the absence of capital controls, interest rates in member countries must remain

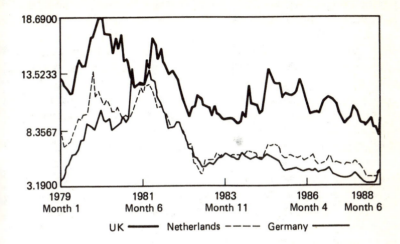

Figure 8.6 Three-month Euromarket interest rates for the UK, the
Netherlands and Germany (annual percentage rates).

'close' together. The Dutch guilder/German mark exchange rate has
been held more or less constant, and the Dutch interest rate follows
that of Germany very closely (see Figure 8.6). Given the small
exchange risk involved in holding guilders rather than marks, only a
small interest rate differential is needed to induce people to switch
assets between the two currencies. Thus when a stable pattern of
exchange rates is expected to be maintained, and when there are no
capital controls, member countries have to have very similar interest
rates. The corollary to this is that only a small interest rate differential is needed to induce large capital flows between them in order, for
example, to finance a large current account deficit or surplus.

8.2.7 Symmetry and asymmetry in the operation of the EMS

A great source of problems with the Bretton Woods system of fixed
exchange rates, which ruled during the period between 1944 and
1971, were two asymmetries in its operation: (a) a deflationary bias,
and (b) the role played by the USA as provider of international
reserves. The intention of the system was that it should have neither
an inflationary nor a deflationary bias. Surplus countries were supposed to take expansionary fiscal and monetary policy action, and
deficit countries to contract. In practice, countries in balance of

payments deficit were obliged to take corrective action, in the form of tight fiscal or monetary policy or ultimately devaluation, whereas the surplus countries were not obliged to take action so promptly and could go on running surpluses and accumulating foreign exchange reserves for long periods of time. This imparted a deflationary bias to the system, and placed most of the burden of adjustment onto deficit countries. The intention of the EMS was to avoid such a bias by giving both of any pair of countries whose bilateral exchange rate reached the edge of the band the obligation to intervene in the foreign exchange markets. The very short-term financing facility was intended to make unlimited quantities of the appreciating currency available to the central bank in the depreciating country for a short period of time with which to defend the parity.

In practice, the experience within Europe since 1979 has been one of deflation. It is a common perception that Germany has resisted any pressure to pursue a more expansionary monetary policy than was consistent with price stability in Germany, and has prevented any exchange market intervention by other countries from having an expansionary effect on German money supply. This may have been a reflection of a common desire among ERM members to reduce inflation, rather than an assertion of German dominance or a source of tension among them. However, recent moves in the EMS have been made to make it operate more symmetrically, and these are described in more detail below.

The second sort of asymmetry in the Bretton Woods system was the ability of the US to ignore its exchange rate, while other countries found that their monetary and fiscal policy was constrained by the need to maintain theirs. This resulted from the simple fact that among n countries there are only $n - 1$ independent exchange rates. Other countries maintained the dollar values of their currencies, and the US did nothing. Whereas other countries found their domestic monetary and fiscal policy subordinated to the need to maintain external balance, the US was able to use those macro policy tools for domestic purposes – to control inflation and employment in the US. The counterpart to this was that US dollars became the international medium of exchange, and the US, as the supplier of dollars, was able to run more or less continuous current account deficits while the rest of the world accumulated dollars with which to finance international payments.

The parallel in the EMS is that other members manage their exchange rates against the German mark by intervening in foreign exchange markets and adjusting interest rates, while Germany can, to a large extent, ignore exchange rates in the EMS. Instead, it uses its monetary policy partly in order to control domestic demand and inflation in Germany, and partly to manage the exchange rate between the mark (and hence the ERM countries as a whole) and other currencies outside the EMS, principally the US dollar and the Japanese yen. So Germany could be said to manage external relations for the ERM countries as a whole. In contrast to the Bretton Woods regime, the dominant country has tended to run surpluses rather than deficits, and the mark is less widely used in the EMS than the dollar was under Bretton Woods as a means of holding foreign exchange reserves and settling international debts. The EC continues to encourage the use of the ECU. There is a growing market for assets denominated in ECUs, as the UK government's recent issue of Treasury bills denominated in ECUs, to the value of several billion pounds, illustrates.

The dominant role of Germany in the ERM has been a source of concern in the EMS, and the concern has grown since inflation rates have converged in Europe. Recent changes in the EMS (described below) have been aimed at making it operate in a more symmetrical way. German dominance has also raised a question about how the system would cope with UK membership. It has been argued that the UK with well-developed international capital markets and no capital controls would rival German leadership in the ERM. Large capital flows between the UK and Germany might, it has been said, destabilise the EMS. Differences of opinion between them about the appropriate level of European exchange rates relative to the US or Japan, about inflation inside European countries, and other causes of disagreement about appropriate monetary and fiscal policy, may trigger such speculative capital flows, and make the EMS susceptible to exchange rate crises. These questions are taken up in more detail in the next section.

8.3   RECENT DEVELOPMENTS IN THE EMS

8.3.1   Strengthening the EMS

As 1992 approaches, and with the intended removal of capital controls in mind, there have been a number of changes made to the EMS intended to make it better able to withstand speculative capital flows, and to make it operate in a more symmetrical way. At a meeting in Nyborg in Denmark in September 1987, EMS finance ministers agreed to take steps (a) to increase monetary policy convergence, and (b) to enhance the resources available to member countries to defend their currencies on the foreign exchange markets.

On convergence, they agreed to implement the macroeconomic 'monitoring procedures' in the EMS which the G7 ('group of 7') countries had already stated their intention of using for global coordination of economic policy. This involves keeping track of a number of economic indicators, including inflation, unemployment, the government budget deficit, the trade balance, interest rates and exchange rates for the EMS countries, and keeping up a series of discussions among countries about their macroeconomic policy, hoping thereby to encourage them to coordinate responses to potential future economic problems. They agreed also to make a 'coordinated and flexible use' of interest rate policies to defend the EMS parity exchange rates. This is a more concrete statement which entails their use of interest rates more vigorously than before. The need for such a policy springs in part from greater freedom of capital movements in the EMS, which forces interest rates of member countries to differ only so as to offset the expected rate of appreciation or depreciation of exchange rates. In the face of large speculative flows, intervention in the foreign exchange markets can have little lasting effect on exchange rates, since the resources available to speculators typically far exceed those available to the central banks. Consequently, the use of interest rates to discourage speculators from moving out of currencies which are expected to depreciate becomes a more important tool of policy.

At the same time as giving more weight to interest rate policy, the ministers also changed the rules on intervention in the EMS. First, they made limited use of the very short–term financing (VSTF) arrangements (described above) available to support intra–marginal intervention. Previously it had been available only for intervention at the margins. Secondly, they made VSTF available for 3½ rather than 2½ months as before. Thirdly, they made loans between central banks under VSTF repayable entirely in ECUs, as against 50 per cent before, for a two-year trial period.

The intention of these changes was to make the EMS more symmetrical. Formerly, countries which had borrowed marks had to repay at least half the loan in marks, which had to be acquired on foreign exchange markets. This limited the extent to which Italian or

French use of DM to defend the lira or franc could affect the German money supply, since the repayment at least in part unwound the initial expansionary effect of the VSTF loan on the stock of DM outstanding. Now Germany is less well able to prevent an automatic increase of its money supply following an episode in which Italy (say) has to defend its currency. Thus any tendency for the mark to appreciate will partly induce a money supply response in Germany which will offset that tendency. It may reduce any bias the system may have towards deflation, and increase the pressure on appreciating countries to expand as well as depreciating countries to contract.

The changes will also formally recognise and encourage the use of intra–marginal intervention by making resources more easily available to central banks. Intra–marginal intervention will, it is hoped, stop currencies from getting to the very edge of the bands, where realignment may seem imminent. This may forestall further speculation.

Capital controls have been gradually removed during the 1980s. Italy and France substantially removed theirs in 1987, though Italy temporarily reversed this. Belgium and Luxembourg still run their two-tier exchange rate system, however. Only Greece, Ireland, Spain and Portugal are now allowed to maintain controls 'on capital movements liberalised under Community law', and these are scheduled for gradual removal over the next few years. The Single European Act gives 31 December 1992 as the date for removing all internal frontiers, including those of capital controls.

8.4   THE EMS AND THE UK

8.4.1   Recent UK monetary policy

During the 1980s there has been a gradual shift in UK monetary policy away from very strict target rates of growth for monetary aggregates towards a more active exchange rate policy. The Medium Term Financial Strategy (MTFS), first outlined in the March 1980 budget, made the reduction of the rate of growth of the £M3 measure of money the central target of macroeconomic policy. Given that the money supply was to be controlled it was not possible to peg the exchange rate simultaneously since any balance of payments surpluses or deficits which resulted would have affected the reserves of the clearing banks and through them the money supply.

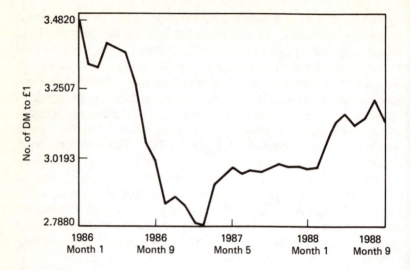

Figure 8.7   £/DM exchange rate.

Source: Datastream.

Although the policy of pursuing monetary targets has never been formally abandoned there is no doubt that it is given far less prominence than it was initially. Instead there seems to have been a move towards active exchange rate policy to make sterling move in line with the deutschmark. Although the rhetoric of government policy remained in terms of monetary control this policy of 'shadowing' the DM was unofficially followed from May 1987 until March 1988. The effects of this can be seen in Figure 8.7 in that the £/DM rate barely deviated from 3 DMs to the pound during this period. However, the abandonment of this policy in March 1988 was followed by a substantial appreciation of the pound.

The logic of the shift from a monetary to an exchange rate target was that monetary control was seen as an increasingly unreliable guide to inflation control. In particular the close relationship between the growth of £M3 and the rate of inflation appeared to break down when the authorities attempted to enforce the MTFS targets. In addition, the failure to pursue any policy of intervention in the foreign exchange market was seen as one of the factors responsible for the rapid appreciation of sterling during the early 1980s which led to a shrinking of the manufacturing base. Tying the exchange rate to a low inflation country such as Germany was seen as a way of maintaining inflationary discipline while avoiding the problems inherent in specifying a target growth rate for a particular monetary aggregate.

Why, given the arguments in the above paragraph, did the UK not simply join the existing EMS system rather than remain officially outside but behave as if it were a member? We cannot provide a definitive answer to this question but we can certainly point to a number of possible considerations.

(a) Having invested a great deal of their credibility in the single-minded pursuit of monetary targets the government has understandably been loathe to acknowledge that this was a mistake or even that the policy is no longer being followed. Since formal membership of the EMS would imply that monetary targets could no longer be maintained it would amount to just such an acknowledgement.

(b) Formal membership of the EMS would imply a loss of freedom of action which informal DM shadowing avoids. One argument is that because of sterling's status as a petrocurrency it is subject to different kinds of external pressures than the other EMS currencies. For example, imagine a fall in the world oil price. Given the current importance of this sector in UK trade this would require a depreciation of the pound. However, such adjustments would be prevented, or at least made more difficult, if the UK was an EMS member.

(c) The UK still has a substantially higher rate of wage inflation than that of the major EMS countries. Thus it would require periodic revaluations if it were not to lose competitiveness steadily. The problem is that given the relatively narrow 2.5 per cent bands these revaluations would probably have to be more frequent than permitted by EMS rules.

Despite the reservations expressed above there would certainly have been some logic in regularising the UK's position within the EMS by acceptance of full membership. However, the possibility of this occurring in 1988 was reduced following the disagreement in the spring between Prime Minister Margaret Thatcher and Chancellor of the Exchequer Nigel Lawson over exchange rate policy. This led to an abandonment of the policy of shadowing the DM. Subsequent monetary policy has involved the use of the rate of interest as a means of keeping the growth of credit and demand in check. The exchange rate is now left to find its own level and consequently has fluctuated in value considerably. The initial appreciation has been argued to have beneficial effects in terms of lower inflation but this may have been only a temporary effect given the subsequent depreciation which has occurred. However, the danger of crowding out of the manufacturing sector of the sort observed in the early 1980s has been averted by the failure of the initial depreciation to be sustained.

8.4.2 Implications for macroeconomic policy

The purpose of this section is to examine the implications for macroeconomic policy of a move to closer monetary union. The traditional instruments of macroeconomic policy are monetary policy exercised either through interest rate control or targeting of monetary aggregates, and fiscal policy exercised through taxation and public spending. The main targets of policy are the maintenance of a low rate of price inflation and the minimisation of short-term fluctuations in the real output of the economy. We might add a third target here in that it is also desirable to avoid persistent balance of payments deficits.

Monetary union can only be achieved in stages. A possible sequence of events would be as follows:

(a) *Stage 1*: Inclusion of the UK within the current EMS system, thus fixing the value of sterling within narrow bands and abolishing controls on international capital movements throughout Europe.
(b) *Stage 2*: Institution of a European central bank with power to determine monetary policies for individual countries as well as a common European monetary policy.
(c) *Stage 3*: Adoption of a common unit of account which would circulate alongside national currencies.
(d) *Stage 4*: Abolition of national currencies in favour of the common unit of account.

Stage 1

Stage 1 represents the sort of strengthening of the EMS which has been proposed for some time. Its implications for the UK would be as follows:

(1) The policy of targeting monetary aggregates could no longer be maintained since monetary policy would have to be formally

geared towards the defence of the exchange rate.

(2) Since exchange rate adjustments could no longer be relied on to maintain competitiveness other policy instruments would have to be directed towards keeping UK prices in line with those of our European competitors. This could take the form of deflationary fiscal policies to offset excessive wage demands or supply-side policies to improve the efficiency of UK industry.

Stage 2

The development of a European central bank is a natural consequence of the closer monetary cooperation described in Stage 1. There are several reasons for this:

(a) So far the EMS has operated using the DM as the key currency with other countries determining their monetary policies with reference to that adopted by the Bundesbank. With the incorporation of the UK into the system there would then be two major international currencies present within the EMS since sterling still has an importance in international markets which is disproportionate to the size of the UK economy. This could lead to competition for the role of key currency within the system which would undermine its effectiveness. A European central bank would be one way of eliminating this destructive tendency, though more explicit international competition might provide an alternative.

　　The Delors report (1989) devotes considerable space to the discussion of the type of central bank which might be formed. It favours a system similar to that in the United States where regional banks cooperate within the Federal Reserve System. The European equivalent would be the European System of Central Banks (ESCB) which would be given the task of organising the monetary policy of the EC as a whole.

(b) Although monetary policy at the national level would no longer be feasible within the EC there would still be the need to formulate an overall European monetary policy to respond to external shocks. For example, it might prove necessary for Europe as a whole to devalue relative to the dollar. Thus a coordinated monetary expansion would have to be engineered. A European central bank would be the natural institutional vehicle by which such policies could be implemented. The Delors report argues that discretionary policy by the ESCB should be

158 John Drifill and Paul Turner

Table 8.1   Inter-European trade 1986 (percentage figures)

	Imports as % of GDP	Imports from EC as % of total imports	Exports to EC as % of total exports
UK	27	52	48
West Germany	27	52	51
France	20	59	55
Italy	18	55	54
Belgium/ Luxembourg	67	72	73
Netherlands	52	75	64
Ireland	53	67	71
Denmark	37	52	47
Greece	30	59	63
Spain	18	50	60
Portugal	41	61	70

Source: IMF Direction of Trade Statistics and International Financial Statistics.

allowed subject to its primary objective of maintaining price stability.

The move towards a European central bank would be a recognition of greater European economic interdependence and part of a more general shift in decision-making towards the European level. This in turn is made necessary by the parallel steps being taken to integrate both product and factor markets by 1992. The extent to which European markets already form an integrated system can be seen in Table 8.1 which shows the extent of the interdependence of the European economies in terms of trade.

Centralised economic decision-making makes sense if all European countries are subject to common external demand disturbances and if there are significant spill-over effects of macroeconomic policy in one country to the rest of Europe. Table 8.1 illustrates that the second of these conditions is likely to hold for the EC. Most member states are relatively open economies in the sense that external trade accounts for a large share of total output. Moreover, a significant fraction of that external trade consists of *inter-European* trade, i.e. imports and exports from, or to, other EC members. This means that expansionary policies by individual countries lead to general expansion throughout the EC through the mechanism of an increase in the exports of the other member states to the expanding country. This reduces the effectiveness of the expansion as perceived at the individual country level but increases it at the aggregate European level.

A well-established result in the theory of economic policy is that when policies have significant effects on other agents the best choices of each individual will yield an outcome which can be improved on by joint action. This is simply a special case of the *prisoner's dilemma* property which is central to game theory. Given that we have established a case for the existence of a large degree of interdependence within the EC it therefore follows that there is a case for supranational policy-making. The argument for a European central bank is that individual central banks cannot be relied on to cooperate since there are incentives to cheat on any agreement reached. For example, suppose all central banks agree on a policy of maintaining low interest rates so as to stimulate growth. It may then be in the interests of each individual bank to increase interest rates slightly, in order to bring down inflation, while relying on the low interest rate policy of the others to maintain the general level of demand. A policy-making institution created specifically to operate at the EC level would have more success in implementing policies which are in the overall interest of the EC members.

Stage 3

The use of a common unit of account has already started to some extent in the form of the ECU. Although this does not circulate widely as an alternative means of exchange it is frequently held by financial institutions as a simple way of hedging against exchange rate fluctuations. If it became feasible for individuals to make use of an alternative to national currencies then this would act as a means of further constraining exchange rates. This is because individuals could always choose to transfer from the national to the EC currency if they felt a devaluation was likely. The only way governments could prevent extreme fluctuations in demand for national currencies would be to keep exchange rates within very narrow bounds. Indeed one consequence could be that national currencies, for which fears of devaluation were persistent, would simply disappear from circulation as residents made use of the safer alternative.

The last point illustrates why governments, particularly those with weaker currencies, may be unwilling to move towards a common monetary unit. Whether or not such a move would be in the overall interests of the EC members depends on whether the gains from greater exchange rate stability outweigh the greater flexibility of action made possible by the existence of separate national currencies.

Stage 4

Finally we conclude with a brief discussion of what the implications of full monetary union, in the form of a single common currency, would be. A common currency would be the logical outcome of the process described above. It represents the ultimate in fixed exchange rate regimes since clearly no realignments are possible if only a single currency exists. There would clearly be problems if realignments are seen as a necessary mechanism for removing regional unemployment by adjusting competitiveness at a regional level. However, these costs would have to be compared to the benefits of having a single means of transactions and reduced instability through exchange rate fluctuations. Whether European countries are willing to adopt such a radical step is by no means clear.

8.5 CONCLUSIONS

In this chapter, we have outlined the structure and operation of the EC, discussed the recent and intended developments of the system, and considered its implications for UK macroeconomic policy. The EMS is in the process of removing remaining exchange controls. This is clearly going to have the effect of tying more closely together the monetary policies of member countries. While the 2.25 per cent bands are maintained, inflation differences between them will have to be accommodated by small (and correspondingly frequent) realignments, implying no discontinuity in the exchange rate. One might envisage, for example, that if French inflation were 2 per cent higher than that of Germany, the franc would be allowed to drift down gradually against the mark, and the parity rate between them realigned at slightly less than annual intervals. This situation ties interest rates of member countries together. To pursue this example, one would expect French interest rates to be about 2 per cent higher than those in Germany to offset the expected exchange rate depreciation. Movements in German rates would be paralleled by movements in French rates, so as to prevent large speculative capital flows. Such a degree of harmonisation of macro policy will require close cooperation among member countries.

A fixed exchange rate between EMS members, in the absence of capital controls, requires that interest rates be more or less uniform throughout the system, and that all countries have the same inflation rate. Countries with higher than average inflation would become increasingly uncompetitive, and those with lower inflation increasingly competitive. Countries which became uncompetitive would have to accept an economic squeeze in order to reduce their production costs relative to those in the rest of the EC. This implies substantial reduction in the freedom of individual countries to pursue independent fiscal and monetary policies. The countervailing gain is the increase in trade, capital and labour mobility, engendered by exchange rate fixity and absence of capital controls. The closer the EMS moves towards fixed rates among members, the more there is a need for a system-wide mechanism for determining its common policy relative to the rest of the world. So far this role has fallen to Germany, but closer ties among members increase the need for a more symmetrical system, and recent changes in the EMS indicate the importance attached to this idea. Such a mechanism would regulate monetary policy in the EMS as a whole, and influence the exchange rate of the ECU relative to the dollar and yen.

UK membership of the exchange rate mechanism of the EMS, means that UK interest rates would be tied more closely to those of Germany and other countries in the system, and the freedom to let the pound appreciate or depreciate against them would be lost. This may imply lower interest rates than have recently prevailed in the UK. It would reinforce the UK government's commitment to zero inflation, and this may of itself reduce inflation expectations in the UK, and hence slow the rate of increase of money wages from the roughly 10 per cent per annum prevailing in mid-1989. Certainly a prolonged period of higher inflation in the UK would cause a progressively tighter squeeze on the UK labour market. Providing the commitment to the EMS was completely credible, there is no reason why balance of trade deficits should be a short-run constraint on the UK economy. Small interest differentials in favour of the pound would be expected to attract sufficient funds from abroad to finance them.

Fiscal policy may have a greater role in influencing demand in the UK in the EMS than it has had in recent years with floating exchange rates. However, the increased openness of the UK economy, envisaged in the single market proposals, implies that any such role is likely to be very limited. Fiscal policy is likely to be guided more by considerations of microeconomic aspects of tax and expenditure policy, smoothing of tax burdens over time, and the maintenance of a desired ratio of national debt to GDP in the medium to long term, rather than short-run demand management considerations.

With 2.25 per cent bands of fluctuation, and starting from an exchange rate of approximately DM 3.20 to the pound, the implied limits of fluctuation would be DM 3.13. to 3.27. Recent experience shows that maintaining sterling within such bounds is not particularly difficult, and may actually imply little change in macro policy in the UK from that which has been in operation in recent years.

The establishment of a common currency and a European central bank still appears to be a very distant prospect, the programme proposed by the Delors report (1989) notwithstanding.

Data Sources

1. *Data on prices and exchange rates*: Monthly figures taken from International Financial Statistics and the EC publication *Eurostatistics*.
2. *Prices*: Consumer prices: general index.
3. *Inflation rates*: Year-on-year increases: $100 \times \log(\mathrm{CPI}(t)/\mathrm{CPI}(t-12))$.
4. *Interest rates*: Three-month Euromarket rates (IFS data).
5. *Data on central rates and the parity grid*: Taken from various issues of the *Bulletin of the Commission of the European Communities*.

Note

1. The Delors report (1989) proposes an extension of the use of the ECU in that it should be used by the ESCB in the conduct of a common monetary policy and that barriers to its private use should be removed. This is consistent with the view of the evolution of a common monetary system which we describe.

References

European Commission, (April 1989) Committee for the Study of Economic and Monetary Union, *Report on Economic and Monetary Union in the European Community*, (Delors Report), Brussels.

Giavazzi, F. and Giovannini, A. (1988) 'The role of the exchange rate regime in a disinflation: empirical evidence on the EMS', in Giavazzi, F., Micossi, S. and Miller, M. (eds), *The European Monetary System*, Cambridge University Press.
van Ypersele, J. and Koeune, J.-C. (1985) *The European Monetary System*, EC Commission, Brussels...

9 The ECU and European Monetary Union

George McKenzie

9.1 INTRODUCTION

My objectives in this chapter are:

(a) to show that the development of a common currency system within the European Monetary System is a necessary condition for the effective completion of the internal European market;
(b) to indicate the steps that will need to be undertaken in order that such a common currency system will be established.

Let us first turn our attention to some fundamental principles.

In order that the international flow of trade and financial items can take place, it is necessary to have some institutional mechanism whereby payments can be made by residents in one country to residents in another. Many such arrangements are possible. At one extreme countries could agree that exchange rates between national currencies should be determined solely by market forces. At the other end of the spectrum there could be a common currency system in which the commercial banking system clears payments between the various countries. An example of this latter scheme is the United Kingdom which operates a common currency system between the four countries: England, Scotland, Wales and Northern Ireland. There is no example of a perfectly flexible exchange rate mechanism. Although today most countries allow some movement in response to market forces, they are usually under the watchful eye of and influenced by frequent intervention of the monetary authorities.

The institutional payments mechanism which the major industrial countries operate today is very much a hybrid, in that two systems are operated in parallel. On the one hand there is the Exchange Rate Mechanism (ERM) of the European Monetary System (EMS), discussed in the previous chapter by Driffill and Turner. This operates very much like the pre-1973 Bretton Woods system of the Inter-

Table 9.1   ECU currency weights and central parities

	Quantity	Central parity
Spanish peseta	6.885	133.631
Irish punt	0.008552	0.767417
Belgian franc	3.431	42.4032
Deutschmark	0.6242	2.05586
Dutch guilder	0.2198	2.31643
French franc	1.332	6.89509
Danish krone	0.1976	7.84195
Italian lira	151.8	1538.24
Sterling	0.08784	0.696904

national Monetary Fund. Such a system involved the maintenance of par value exchange rates for prolonged periods of time and a band around the par within which rates were flexible. The second part of the hybrid system involves countries like the US and Japan which allow the market to influence exchange rate movements between themselves and with the currencies of the ERM. It is not a completely flexible system in that the monetary authorities intervene to dampen down fluctuations when these are considered to be excessively volatile.

When the EMS was formally established on 1 January 1979, it was apparent that it was to be more than simply a mechanism whereby its members would regulate their exchange rates. A central feature of the system would be the creation of the European Currency Unit or ECU. This is a composite monetary unit in the sense that it consists of officially agreed amounts of the currencies of the EMS member countries. The amounts involved are shown in Table 9.1. These quantities are not immutably fixed and since 1979 there have been changes in the ECU basket of currencies.

According to the enabling resolution of the European Council of 5 December 1978, the ECU would be used

(a) as the denominator (*numéraire*) for the exchange rate mechanism;
(b) as the basis for a divergence indicator;
(c) as the denominator for operations in both the intervention and the credit mechanism;
(d) as a means of settlement between monetary authorities of the EC.

In other words, the ECU would serve both as a means of payment and a unit of account for the monetary authorities of EMS members. In principle, these 'official' ECUs could be created simply by fiat and allocated to countries according to their importance in international trade and finance. However, the EC opted for an arrangement whereby the ECU would be partially backed. Each member, including the United Kingdom, is required to deposit 20 per cent of its gold reserves and 20 per cent of its dollar reserves with the European Monetary Co-operation Fund (EMCF). In return each country receives an equal value of ECUs. Each monetary authority is obliged to intervene in foreign exchange markets so as to keep the actual market exchange rate close to the central rate. At present the band is ±2.25 per cent for France, Germany, Italy, the Netherlands, Belgium, Luxembourg and Denmark. The UK operates with a band of ±6 per cent.

9.2 THE EUROPEAN MONETARY SYSTEM IN 1990

The central objective of the 1992 directives and EC policy is to create an economic environment within which all member countries operate on a level pegging. In the jargon of the day, everyone should be on a level playing field, ideally, operating under the same tax systems with the same competition policy and, in general, having unimpeded access to final goods, intermediate input, raw materials, labour and finance on the same terms. The resulting increase in cross-border competition will cause the most efficient firms to expand. Employment opportunities will increase and consumers will enjoy lower prices.

However, such gains are not costless. Something must be given up and in this case each EC member country must sacrifice some degree of sovereignty. Previous chapters have noted that control over competition policies, trade policies, health and safety regulations, the cross-border movement of financial assets, *et al.*, will shift away from national regulatory agencies to bodies directly responsible to the European Commission. The same is also true of the operation of monetary and fiscal policies. It is here that the UK has faced a significant dilemma. Prior to 1990 when the UK was not a member of the ERM, sterling fluctuated in value to a greater extent than is allowed today. The advantage of this greater flexibility was that it allowed the Bank of England greater autonomy in the execution of monetary policy. The disadvantage is that such flexibility creates an environment of uncertainty which increases costs to foreign traders and international investors. This uncertainty acts very much like a tariff and increases the cost of both traded goods and finance. However, eliminating this cost would mean abandoning heavy reliance upon monetary policy to achieve domestic economic policy objectives. Let us examine these points in detail.

9.2.1 UK monetary policy under a flexible exchange rate system

Let us suppose that the Bank of England had decided to follow a restrictive monetary policy prior to Britain's entry into the ERM. As a consequence UK interest rates rise relative to those abroad. This causes adjustments in both the financial and real sectors. On the one hand, the demand for sterling increases as investors seek to take advantage of the higher yields and hence the pound appreciates. On the other hand, the productive sector of the UK economy will be affected by both the interest rate and exchange rate changes. The higher interest rates should damp down aggregate expenditure whereas the exchange rate appreciation will shift demand away from British produced goods towards those abroad. The net result will be a decline in output. The opposite result would occur if the Bank of England followed an expansionary monetary policy. The conclusion to be reached is that a system of flexible exchange rates and domestic stabilisation based on monetary policy would appear to be complementary.

However, there is a cost. Because there will normally be a lag between the placement of an order for imported goods and the actual delivery when payment is made, both importers and exporters will be concerned about the possibility of adverse exchange rate movements during this period. For example, suppose that a German importer purchases £100,000 worth of goods from the UK with payment due in three months. If the current exchange rate of DM 3 per £ remains unchanged the goods will cost the importer DM300,000. However, if the pound should appreciate against the deutsch mark, say to DM 4 per £, then the imports would cost DM400,000. Such variability in exchange rates will in turn lead to variability in profit levels and/or prices. Faced with such uncertainty, German importers may find it more convenient to produce for domestic markets or for export to EMS countries whose exchange rates are relatively stable. The effects of such uncertainty act like a tariff on trade in that they impose a potential cost on foreign traders. Of course, it would have been possible for the German exporter to arrange with his bank to sell the £100,000 forward at an exchange rate agreed today when the pounds are delivered in three months time. But such a service involves a cost both in terms of the fee which the bank will charge and in terms of the manpower which the company's finance officer must devote to managing its foreign currency exposure. There is a further problem. It is difficult to arrange forward contracts which cover a period longer than a year. Consequently aircraft companies may have to maintain open foreign currency positions and make provisions in pricing agreements to cover the cost of any adverse exchange rate movements. However, inevitably that will mean that they appear less competitive than foreign producers, at least in so far as export markets are concerned.

Now that the UK is a member of the ERM, exchange rates and interest rates should be less volatile than they were under the system of flexibility. This follows from the fact that exchange rates are constrained within a band of plus or minus 2.6 per cent of a central parity rate. However, just as there are problems with a flexible exchange rate system so there are problems with the way the EMS is managed. Specifically, the monetary authorities of EMS countries intervene in such a way as to perpetuate disequilibria in financial markets, and especially the foreign exchange markets.

9.2.2 Disequilibria in the EMS

To understand how these disequilibria are created, we begin by examining the balance sheet of a representative central bank. Since any transaction always involves two entries by double-entry accounting practice, the following balance sheet of a central bank:

Central Bank Balance Sheet

Assets	Liabilities
Securities (DC)	Notes and coins held by public (NCP)
Net foreign asset position (NFAP)	Commercial bank reserves (CBR)

can also be represented by the identity:

$$DC + NFAP \equiv NCP + CBR$$

Suppose that this country suffers an overall balance of payments deficit. That is, there is an excess demand for foreign currency. (This is equivalent to an excess supply of the domestic currency.) If the exchange rate is fixed (or within the relatively narrow band of the ERM) then the monetary authority must satisfy this excess demand by selling some of its holding of foreign currencies. In terms of the central bank's balance sheet NFAP falls. Since those buying the foreign currency are selling domestic currency to the monetary authority, the effect is very much like a restrictive monetary policy. If the monetary authority's holdings of securities (DC) remains unchanged then notes and coins (NCP) and bank reserves (BR) must both decline. The resulting fall in liquidity and bank credit would lead to a reduction in aggregate expenditure, including imports. This process would continue until the international payments imbalance was eliminated.

Changes in aggregate demand usually lead to corresponding changes in employment levels in the short run. For that reason, governments do not like to see the above adjustment process take place. As NFAP falls as in the above example, an offsetting open-market operation is undertaken such that DC rises. The converse would happen if there was a balance of payments surplus. Because aggregate spending remains at its initial level, any international payments imbalance continues with the result that some countries will appear to be in persistent deficit whereas others will appear to be in persistent surplus. The monetary authorities in the former group will find their international reserve position deteriorating whereas those in the latter group will find it improving. Inevitably, such a disequilibrium situation as induced by the monetary authorities can only continue for so long, either until the deficit countries run out of reserves or the surplus countries are no longer willing to lend to them. Perceiving that this is the situation, speculators act in such a way as to compound the pressure by selling the currency of the deficit country in exchange for the currencies of surplus countries. It is a one-way bet.

These sources of uncertainty can be eliminated by the creation of a common currency system throughout Europe. But first there must exist a stock of assets denominated in ECUs and widely traded throughout the European Community. Such assets will ensure that smooth financial adjustments take place within the common currency area. In addition, they will act as the vehicle for the execution of open-market operations by the union's monetary authority. It is exactly these roles which US Treasury securities fulfil within the US monetary system. To understand what is involved we need to develop further our analysis of the automatic payments adjustments mechanism which characterises a monetary union.

9.3 AUTOMATIC ADJUSTMENT WITHIN A COMMON CURRENCY SYSTEM

Those regions or countries which have a balance of payments deficit are spending more than they are earning abroad. Cash balances will fall and credit will become less available. As a result interest rates will increase. Just the opposite will occur in surplus regions and countries. Cash balances will rise, credit will be more available and interest rates will fall. Expenditure will decline in the deficit country and rise in the surplus country. The flow of investment funds from the latter to the former will slow down but not offset the adjustment. A process of gradual change takes place.

However, the scenario just described presumes that the financial markets of those countries belonging to a monetary union are highly integrated. Consider the monetary union of the 50 American states. Will investors as far away as the states of Maine or New Hampshire be willing to move their funds to California to take advantage of the higher yield which may exist there? The same question could be asked of investors in Denmark and Greece or in any other of the EMS countries. The basic problem is one of information availability. Many investors will be uncertain as to economic conditions prevailing in California. They will be cautious about moving funds from locally issued financial instruments about whose performance they may have first-hand knowledge. However, within the United States the existence of a large stock of widely held government debt acts as a vehicle for arbitrage. As interest rates rise in California, asset holders there will rearrange their portfolios by selling US government debt in favour of the higher yielding local assets. This has the effect of driving up yields on the government debt. Asset holders in Maine now find that yields on government debt are high relative to those of local assets. As they rearrange their portfolios yields rise in Maine.

Further, because the asset is widely held, it ensures that the impact of contractionary or expansionary open-market operations are spread throughout the monetary union.

The process just described is crucial to the smooth operation of a monetary union. Cash balances do not immediately fall by the full amount of the trade imbalance in the deficit region. Nor do they rise by the full amount of the trade imbalances of the surplus regions. The operation of the market mechanism acts to ensure an adjustment process which does not inhibit the growth or efficiency of the productive sector.

In principle, such a process could work within the EMS provided, of course, that there are no restrictions on the international flow of funds. Then the issue becomes one of identifying an asset which is widely held throughout the European Community and could act as a link between the financial markets of Denmark and Greece as well as the major European financial centres. Ironically, such an asset already exists: the dollar; the Eurocurrency system currently plays a key role in linking the financial markets of Europe. For example, consider the following scenario. If interest rates were to rise in the UK, asset holders would reduce the level of their dollar deposits at UK banks in favour of sterling assets. This would cause yields to rise on Eurodollar deposits thereby attracting funds from Germany, France and other European countries. Cash balances would fall in the latter and their interest rates would rise.

If this process were to form the basis of the international adjustment process within the EMS, then some hard decisions will have to be made. If the dollar were to remain the link between European financial centres, then coordination of interest rate and exchange rate policies by both the European monetary union and North America would be paramount. Otherwise the uncertainties associated with a flexible exchange rate system or the adjustable parity of the EMS would always be in the background. One solution would be to create a North Atlantic Monetary System. However, recently Japanese financial institutions have rapidly expanded their operations within both North America and Europe. Because of its increased interdependence with these financial centres, it is logical that Japan should also be a member of any monetary union involving the major industrial trading nations. At this point in time, it is unlikely that such a scenario is viable. Neither the United States nor Japan is likely to forego sovereignty over monetary policy that membership in a monetary union would entail.

Table 9.2   External positions in European Currency Units of banks reporting to the Bank for International Settlements (in billions of US dollars)

	December 1986	December 1987	December 1988
Bank assets:			
Total	55.9	77.7	86.0
of which residents hold	20.1	27.6	32.6
Non-bank sector	10.4	15.3	16.0
Banking sector	44.8	62.4	70.0
Bank liabilities:			
Total	48.4	66.3	76.9
of which residents hold	16.3	20.3	27.1
Non-bank sector	3.2	4.7	4.9
Banking sector	45.2	61.6	72.0

Source: Bank for International Settlements, International Banking and Financial Market Developments.

The political reality of the situation poses a problem for the United Kingdom which is highly vulnerable to fluctuations in (a) the price of petroleum (which is denominated in dollars) and (b) US interest rates. Both of these variables are outside the control of EMS countries and the United Kingdom. However, because the UK is an important oil producer and a major financial entrepôt, it is more vulnerable to the effects of developments within these sectors. At the moment its financial interests would appear to lie more in North America than in Europe. For this reason it has a strong reason to prefer exchange rate flexibility with the exchange rate absorbing some of the external shocks.

9.4   THE ADVANTAGES OF THE ECU

There is an alternative. The European Monetary System could create its own widely held financial asset. The growth in private market European Currency Units would appear to be a promising development in this direction. These private ECUs created by banks have the same structure as those officially created by the EMS. As can be seen from Table 9.2, there has been a steady growth in the stocks of private ECUs although these are held primarily by banks. The

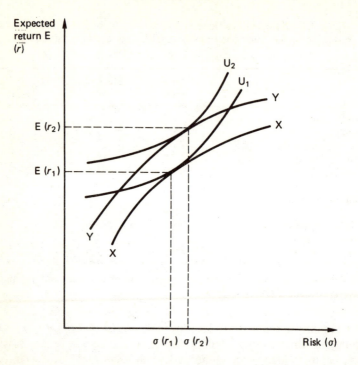

Figure 9.1 Development of the ECU as a medium of exchange.

question then arises as to what developments are required in order to enhance the role of the ECU in European trade and finance.

In principle, the recent development of the private ECU market is particularly important. Since the ECU is a weighted average of EMS currencies, it is an attractive asset in which to hold European foreign currency assets. A depreciation in one member's currency *vis-à-vis* the other partners will entail a relatively small capital loss with respect to ECU assets compared to the loss involved if all assets were denominated in the depreciating currency. Transactions in ECUs provide an effective means of hedging. In addition, they have the advantage that they could be used as a medium of exchange, i.e. they could be used for transactions purposes.

The implications of such a development are illustrated in Figure 9.1. On the vertical axis, we plot the expected returns which would be generated by alternative portfolios of assets which might include dollar, sterling and ECU financial items as well as assets denominated in other currencies. On the horizontal axis is plotted the risk associated with such portfolios. The schedule XX represents the highest expected returns which could be achieved given any level of risk, where the portfolio does not include ECU-denominated assets. Note (a) that higher expected returns can only be achieved at the cost of higher risk, and (b) that risk is an increasing rate relative to return. We assume that asset preferences are represented by a set of indifference curves, two of which are shown in Figure 9.1. Investors are assumed to be risk averse. Given XX, the optimal portfolio will be consistent with expected return $E(r)$ and risk $\sigma(r)$. However, the existence of ECU-denominated assets can improve the efficiency of the financial system. This is reflected in an upward shift in the set of feasible opportunities from XX to YY. The reason for this is that the ECU enables investors to spread their risks across a market of currencies. To the extent that the ECU can also be used as a medium of exchange, the brokerage charges involved in switching in and out of various currencies are eliminated.

9.5   A POTENTIAL PROBLEM

Nevertheless, it is the case that ECUs in their current state of development could actually represent a threat to the evolution of the European Monetary System. Consider the example illustrated by the hypothetical balance sheets shown in Figure 9.2. Let us suppose that a British resident, individual A, believes that his financial objectives could be better achieved by increasing the proportion of his assets denominated in ECUs. A sells sterling and buys ECUs which are held at a bank (here denoted the Eurobank) prepared to accept deposits in this currency of denomination. The Eurobank now possesses additional ECU funds which can be lent, in our example to individual B, say a Belgian resident. B exchanges the ECUs for Belgian francs and purchases goods from another Belgian resident C. The net result is a decline in cash balances in the UK and an increase in cash balances in Belgium. If we consolidated the balance sheets of the UK and Belgian banks we determine that there is no net change in their total liabilities. However, additional liquidity and credit has been created via the intermediation of the Eurobank. As a result, the total assets and liabilities of the European banking system have increased. It should be noted that this situation is analogous to that which has characterised the growth of Eurodollar deposits over the

UK bank		Eurobank	
Bank reserves:	Account of individual A:	Loan to individual B:	Account of individual A:
−£100	−£100	+200 ECUs	+200 ECUs

Individual A transfers funds from his UK bank to the Eurobank which, in turn, lends ECUs to individual B. The latter exchanges his ECUs for Belgium francs and buys goods from individual C.

Belgian bank

Bank reserves: +BFr 7,000	Account of individual C: +BFr 7,000

Figure 9.2   A hypothetical set of transactions involving ECUs (assuming £1 = 2 ECU = 70 Belgian francs).

past forty years. In each case the deposits are 'backed' by the credit which the Eurobank has extended.

To the extent that ECUs are reasonably close substitutes for any existing national currency, say sterling, then the liquidity preference schedule for sterling will shift to the left and become more elastic, as shown in Figure 9.3. Interest rates will decline from r_1 to r_2 thereby stimulating additional expenditure, even with an unchanged monetary base. Further, attempts to influence UK interest rates will now require larger changes in the money supply than was the case before the ECU came into existence.

The implication is that the successful evolution of the EMS will require the inclusion of the ECU in the national monetary aggregates designed to measure overall bank liabilities and credit. To prevent an uncontrolled monetary expansion, any time there is an increase in ECU bank deposits there must be an offsetting decrease in domestic currency deposits. This can be achieved by requiring that commercial banks hold reserves against ECU liabilities in the same manner that they hold reserves against domestic currency deposits. And such ECU bank reserves would need to be counted as part of a country's monetary base.

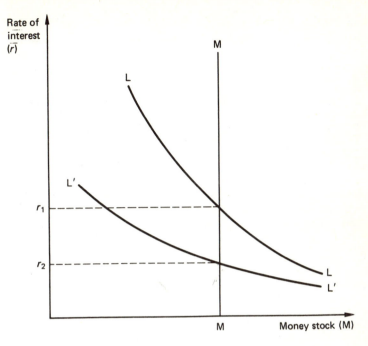

Figure 9.3   Effect of ECUs as a substitute for national currencies.

The stakes are quite high. In recent years there has been a considerable amount of variability in exchange rates and, as a consequence, in national interest rates. The reasons for this variability are a matter of debate amongst economists. It may be due to the execution of monetary and fiscal policies in the United States and various European countries, or it might be due to the misperceived expectations of future interest and exchange rate movements in the money markets. Needless to say a monetary union based on a common currency system would face none of these difficulties. By definition such a system eliminates exchange rate risk between the member nations although such risks would still exist *vis-à-vis* the currencies of non-members. As a result relative interest rates will be stable. This can be shown by referring to the experience of monetary unions such as the USA, UK and Germany where regional interest rate differentials are small and relatively stable. This is important because exchange rate and interest rate uncertainty over five- to ten-year horizons can act as a significant deterrent to long-run investment.

George McKenzie

Table 9.3   Advantages of and obstacles to using ECU for invoicing

| | Answers | | Mean |
	Number	%	position
Advantages:			
Simplified admin. and management:			
– in commercial operations	33	33.0	1.85
– in foreign exchange and			
Treasury management	78	78.0	1.32
– in intergroup accounting	11	11.0	2.55
Reduced exchange risk:			
– less resort to price revision clauses	42	42.0	2.14
– improved competitiveness	30	30.0	2.60
– more flexible settlement terms	24	24.0	2.67
– Other	12	12.0	2.33
– No answer	4	–	
Total current and future users	100	100.0	
Obstacles:			
– Lack of information	79	38.7	1.75
– Unacceptable to partner	136	66.7	1.41
– Over-complex management	22	10.7	2.36
– Geographical concentration of			
foreign trade	23	11.27	1.87
– Raw materials not quoted in ECU	73	35.8	2.21
– Possibility never considered	55	27.0	2.02
– Restrictive regulations	13	6.4	3.00
– Other	27	13.2	1.96
– No answer	8	–	
Total	204	100.0	

NB: Mean position is calculated on 5 possible answers.

Source: *ECU Newsletter*, January 1986.

9.6   PROSPECTS FOR THE FUTURE

For the European Currency Unit to form the basis for a Common Currency System, it must

(a) be accepted as a currency for invoicing;
(b) be accepted as a means of payment;
(c) be the currency of denomination of assets widely accepted throughout the EMS;

Table 9.4   Advantages and obstacles to using ECU for foreign trade financing

	Answers		Mean position
	Number	*%*	*position*
Advantages:			
– Lower rates	35	43.7	1.86
– Lower effective cost of financing	57	71.2	1.53
– Stabler interest rate	39	48.7	2.65
– Stabler exchange rate	54	67.5	2.19
– Alternative to forward hedging	12	15.0	2.42
– Simplified treasury management	6	7.5	2.83
– Other	2	2.5	4.00
– No answer	–	–	
Total regular users	80	100.0	
Obstacles:			
– Lack of information	35	28.2	1.46
– Difficult to obtain	2	1.6	2.00
– Complex treasury management	4	3.2	1.75
– Preference for currency used to invoice	61	49.2	1.16
– Possibility never considered	14	11.3	1.50
– Other	25	20.3	1.32
– No answer	8	–	
Total non-users	124	100.0	

NB: Mean position is calculated on 5 possible answers.

Source: *ECU Newsletter*, January 1986.

For (a) and (b) to be satisfied it must be the case that both producers and consumers perceive it to be in their interest to use the ECU. It is already used in some instances but not very widely in comparison to national currencies. At the moment, the situation is not clear-cut. Users and potential users perceive that there exist both advantages and disadvantages to using the ECU. Consider Tables 9.3 and 9.4. In general, it is perceived that use of the ECU would lead to simplified financial management and reduction of exchange rate risk. A major disadvantage is that not all (or even most) of a companies' trading partners and customers will be using it or find it convenient to accept ECUs.

One possible strategy for increasing the use of the ECU is for the governments of the EMS countries to utilise it in their transactions with the private sector. A step in this direction occurred in August

1988 when the UK Treasury repaid before maturity 2.5 billion dollars of floating rate notes and refinanced a portion of these in ECUs. The issue was oversubscribed indicating that there does exist substantial unsatisfied demand for ECU-denominated assets. If other governments were to restructure their debt into ECUs there would then gradually develop the market for a widely accepted, relatively safe asset throughout the EC. This would then perform the linking role that Treasury bills play in the United States, as discussed earlier, and enable a European central bank to undertake open-market operations with a view towards controlling liquidity and bank credit within the EMS.

Index

182 *Index*

Cars cont.

standards for 39
Cassils de Dijon case (1978) 40
Caves, R. 21, 24n
Cecchini, P. 6n, 24n, 29, 36, 38, 41-4,
47-9, 129, 135n
Chalkley, M.J. 107, 122n
Channel Tunnel 116
chemical products 2, 11, 13, 20, 46
cigarettes, excise duties on 74, 85
clothing 14-15, 76
industry 11, 13
Cnossen, S. 76, 97n
Cockfield Programme 36, 48
colour televisions 37, 39, 46
commodity taxes 94-7
in a federal system 88-94
in a single closed economy 78, 81,
84
see also indirect taxes
Common Agricultural Policy 28, 93-4
common currency 5-6, 134-5, 137-8,
144, 156, 160, 162, 165, 171-3,
177
see also European Currency Unit;
European Monetary System
company taxation, harmonisation of
71
competition, increased 2-6, 17, 23
as a result of reduction in trade
barriers 61-3, 69
Completing the Internal Market
(Commission of the European
Communities-1985) 71, 75, 97n
Completion of the European Market
(Commission of the European
Communities-1987) 71, 73-5
computing equipment x
construction 2, 13, 49
consumer electronics-France (CE)
45-6

Cooke Committee of the Bank for
International Settlements 126-7
Council of Ministers 29-31, 44
qualified majority voting 1, 30, 40,
48
see also European Commission
Cowling, K. 21, 24n
cross-border shopping 90-1
customs procedures 10-11, 51
see also border controls; frontier
controls

data processing 13
Davies, S. 21, 24n
defence industries 23, 41, 43
defence spending 11-12
Delors, Jacques 29, 45, 48, 49
Committe Report (1989) xii, 6,
137-8, 157-8, 162
demand elasticities 16, 63
Denmark 15, 18, 71, 128, 158, 166-7,
172
and the ERM 139
excise duties 74
VAT rates 73
Deutsche Industrie-Norm (DIN) 38
diesel, excise duties on 74
Digby, C. 68, 69n
Directives (to achieve completion of
the Internal Market) xi, 1-5, 31,
48, 128, 167
drug trafficking 97

Economic and Monetary Affairs
Committee 85
Economics of 1992, The (Commission
of the European Communities-1988)
2-3, 6n, 11-20, 24n, 53-4, 55,
59-60, 69n, 135n
economies of scale x, 2-4, 9, 18,
19-23, 32, 34, 43, 61-3, 69, 99,
110
in financial services 132-3
in high-tech industries 13
electric motors 20, 62, 65-6
electrical engineering 11
electrical goods 13, 62, 65
electromagnetic compatibility 49
electronics 13, 18
employment
in Britain 100, 104-11, 120-2

Netherlands, cont.

VAT rates 73
Newly Industrialised Countries (NICs) 35
Nickell, S.J. 104, 110, 122n
Nicolaides, P. 15, 24n
Nissan 37
non-metal mineral products 11
non-tariff barriers (NTBs) 4, 15, 51
    categories of 27-9
    costs of 27, 32-5
    instruments for removing 29-31
    overall picture 47-50
    role of private firms 45-7
    tackling NTBs in practice 35-45
    see also frontier controls; public procurement; technical standards; transport regulations

office machinery 13, 62, 65
Official Journal of the European Community 41, 56
Oulton, N. 21, 24n
Owen, N. 34, 50n

Padoa-Schioppa, T. 46, 50n
paper industry 11, 20
Pearson, M. 73-5, 76, 97n
Pelkmans, J. 44, 50n, 54
persons, free movement of 2, 49
    see also labour market
Petrofina xi
petrol, 173
    excise duties on 74
pharmaceuticals 2, 11, 13, 54-5, 65-6
    prices of 15-16
Philips 34, 39, 46
Pissarides, C.A. 104, 107, 111, 119, 122n
plastic industry 11
Plessey 31
Portugal
    capital movements 124-5, 153
    excise duties 74
    inter-European trade 158
    VAT rates 73

power generation 41, 43
Prais, S. 21, 25n
precision engineering 11
precision equipment 11, 13
pressure vessels 49
Price, S. 104, 122n
Price Waterhouse 129-32
production, restrictions affecting 2-3
professions
    free movement of 2, 99, 119-20
    recognition of qualifications 99, 119
protectionism 66-9, 84
public authorities
    contracts 41-5, 56
    purchases by 41-5, 55-6
public procurement 2, 4, 11-12, 17, 18, 23, 49
    and hidden subsidies 41-5
    effects of removal 55-6
public sector bodies 12, 55-6
    see also public authorities

railway equipment x, 12
    locomotives 43
refrigerators 38
Regional Fund 94
Renault 34
research and development (R&D) 13, 17
restaurant meals, taxation on 90-1, 96
Rossini, G. 15, 25n
Rover 34
rubber products 11

Scherer, F.M. 20, 25n
Schmalensee, R. 45, 50n
Second Banking Co-ordination Directive-Jan 1988 126
securities 2, 5, 128-9
segmented markets 62-6, 69
Shoup, C. 76, 97n
Smith, A. 61-6, 68, 69n
Smith, Adam 2
Smith, S. 73-5, 76, 97n
Sony 39
sovereignty, loss of ix, 6, 134, 137, 167-8